The All New Yeast Free Cooking

by Glori Winders

Published by Glori Winders

©2014, Glori Winders (CS1/KDP1)
7th Edition
ISBN: 978-1500971915

Special Note About Book Formatting

If you are reading this book in print form then you should have no issues, however, if you are reading an eBook format then please read this special note.

I love reading cookbooks. I love collecting cookbooks. I LOVE COOKBOOKS!

Over the years I have collected hundreds of printed cookbooks and they give me comfort to sit and read them. They bring back memories of family dinners or special occasions.

As my husband and I began to travel more and stay for extended periods of time away from home I missed my cookbooks. I began to purchase new cookbooks as eBooks. And, many times I was very disappointed. The formatting would be wrong and the book difficult to read.

I did not realize until I began writing cookbooks myself how much of a challenge formatting eBooks can be. I have made every effort and spent countless hours working on templates that would make my cookbooks easy to use on any Reader. However, you have some control over the way the content looks. Most Readers give you the ability to choose background colors and font sizes. All of these changes can totally change the layout of an eBook.

With my cookbooks, you should be able to use any font size and read the book from vertical or horizontal perspective. But, there are so many formats and so many Readers I can not guarantee that this book will work perfectly on every device. I do apologize if you have any problems. I like for things to be perfect. But, this is one battle where I have had to wave the white flag.

In my opinion the best way to use this cookbook in the kitchen is vertical (up and down) and Scrolling instead of Page Turning (if your Reader gives you this option). This ensures that you can have an entire recipe on one page while you are cooking.

I hope this bit of information helps you and makes your reading and use of this book more enjoyable.

YOU HAVE BEEN **GLORI**-FIED

Table of Contents

How To Use This Cookbook — 13

General Guidelines For Using This Cookbook — 14

Cooking & Baking with Alternative Whole Grains — 17

What To Eat The First Three Weeks — 19

Foods You Can Eat Freely — 19

Foods You Can Eat Cautiously — 21

Foods You Must Avoid Completely — 22

What To Drink — 23

What To Drink Freely — 23

Drinks To Avoid — 23

Your Symptoms — 24

Four Stages In Controlling Your Symptoms — 24

The Steps — 24

Appetizers, Starters & Snacks — 27

Better Than Crackers — 28

Crispy Tortilla Threads — 29

Egg Rolls Without The Roll — 30

Eggplant Balls — 31

Falafel — 32

Rosemary Lemon Popcorn — 33

Beverages — 35

Fresh Tomato Juice — 36

Sparkling Lemonade — 37

Breads	**39**
Applesauce Bread	40
Baking Mix	41
Baking Mix Biscuits	42
Baking Mix Cornbread	43
Baking Mix Mexican Cornbread	44
Baking Mix Muffins	45
Banana Bread	46
Old Fashioned Corn Cakes	47
Chowders, Soups & Stews	**49**
Basic UnCanned Condensed Soup	50
Broccoli Soup	51
Caramelized Roasted Fennel Soup	52
Corn & Crab Chowder	53
Fresh & Quick Tomato Soup	55
Gumbo	56
Irish Stew	58
Large Batch Condensed Cream of Celery Soup	59
Large Batch Condensed Cream of Chicken Soup	60
Quick & Savory Chili	61
Roasted Red Pepper Soup	62
The Best Split Pea Soup	63
Tortilla Soup	64
Tuscan White Bean Soup	65
Dessert	**67**

Hot Toffee In A Mug	68
Cocoa Bark	69
Apple Crisp	70
Creamy Custard	71
Creamy Eggless Rice Pudding	72
Instant Rice Pudding with Cinnamon	73
Lemon Custard	74
Melt In Your Mouth Shortbread	75
Dips, Dressings & Sauces	**77**
Creamy Cucumber Dressing	78
Fresh Salsa	79
Garlic Vinaigrette	80
Guacamole	81
Homemade Mayonnaise	82
Hummus	83
Japanese Style Ginger Dressing	84
Lemon Tarragon Aioli	85
Olive Oil Dipping Sauce	86
Quick & EZ Tomato Sauce	87
Roasted Vegetable Dip	88
Spicy Pear Sauce	89
Tomato Italian Herb Dressing	90
Meats	**91**
Beef Fajitas	92
Beef Lo Mein	94

Braised Beef, Peppers & Onions: Ropa Vieja Style	95
Dry Rubbed Flank Steak	97
Garlic & Ghee Pinwheel Steaks	98
Homemade Breakfast Sausage	99
Homemade Italian Sausage	100
Homemade Polish Kielbasa	102
Jamaican Jerk Flank Steak	103
Oriental London Broil	104
Peppercorn Steak	105
Swiss Steak	106
Tamale Pie	107
Poultry	**109**
Chicken with 20 Cloves of Garlic	110
Chicken Drummers	111
Chicken Fajitas	112
Chicken with Sage	114
Deep-Fried Cajun Turkey	115
French Inspired Chicken	116
Honey Lime Chicken	117
Stir-Fried Chicken & Vegetables	118
Salads	**119**
Baby Black Lentil Salad	120
Bite Sized Veggie Salad	121
Evelyn's Potato Shrimp Salad	122
Mixed Greens with a Lime Vinaigrette	123

Nancy's French-Style Green Bean Salad	124
Pimento Corn Salad	125
Simple Avocado Salad	126
Taco Salad	127
Seafood	**129**
Awesome Shrimp on the Barbie	130
Perfect Salmon & Potatoes	131
Spicy Seared Scallops	133
Steamed Alaskan King Crab Claws	134
Super Fast Fire Fish	135
The Family's Favorite Fish & Potatoes	136
Seasonings	**137**
Cajun Seasoning	138
Chili Powder	139
Curry Powder	140
Ghee	141
Seafood Seasoning	142
Southwest Seasoning	143
Spice Mix for Grilled Vegetables	144
Taco Seasoning	145
Starches	**147**
Basic Polenta	148
Bean Thread Noodles	149
Brown & Wild Rice Pilaf	150
Fried Rice	151

Fried Sweet Potato Chips	152
Garlic Rice	153
Green Onion Hash Brown Potatoes	154
Mashed Sweet Potatoes	155
Saffron Rice	156

Tips & Tricks — 157

Alcohol & Liqueur Substitutions	158
Fruit & Vegetable Wash	159
Lemon or Lime Juice Cubes	160
Omelet Kits	161
Pumpkin Seeds	162
Ready To Use Ground Beef	163
Yogurt Cheese	164
Yummy Chicken Stock	165

Vegetables — 167

Acorn Squash Gone Hawaiian	168
Crunchy Snow Pea Sauté	169
Eggplant and the Sea	170
Glazed Carrots with Shallots & Thyme	171
Grilled Asparagus with Lemon & Garlic	172
Hoppin' John - It's A Southern Thing!	173
Indian-Style Vegetable Stir Fry	174
Oven Dried Tomatoes	175
Quick & Easy Refried Beans	176
Ratatouille	177

Roasted Cauliflower	178
Spicy Broccoli	179
Tangy Brussels Sprouts	180
Vegetables Fried in Brown Rice Batter	181
Zucchini Noodles	182
Resources	**183**
Converting To Metrics	**185**
Weight Conversions	185
Volume Conversions	185
Temperature Conversions	186
About Glori	**187**
A Note From Glori	**188**
Discover Other Titles by Glori	**189**
Connect With Glori	**189**
My Special Gift To You	**190**

Chapter 1

How To Use This Cookbook

General Guidelines For Using This Cookbook

There are a few basic rules that you will need to follow when using this cooking manual. Remember that the goal is to avoid yeast. Yeast and molds can build up very quickly on foods. Because of this you should avoid leftovers as much as possible. If you do eat leftovers, heat them really well to kill the yeast and molds.

Also, remember that I am not a physician. So, if there is an ingredient listed that your doctor has told you not to eat, then don't eat it. There are quite a few different thoughts as to what you should not eat when avoiding yeast. I know that these recipes work, because I am living proof. However, do what your doctor has told you to do.

As far as ingredients, please use the following substitutions & guidelines:

As a general rule Stage 1 recipes can be used anytime. Stage 2 recipes should be used sparingly once your yeast problem is under control.

If we lived in a perfect world then all of our veggies would be homegrown, fresh and wonderful. However, I live in the real world. I know that it is hard to get fresh ingredients at times, so I have used a few canned items. Avoid canned food as much as possible and read labels very carefully to make sure that there are not sugars and preservatives added.

When a recipe calls for salt, I use Real Salt® brand salt. You can also use sea salt, but make sure that there are no additives and it has not been bleached.

Never use dried fruit. It is covered in molds that you can not see with the human eye.

Bragg's Amino Acids are a perfect substitute for soy or Worcestershire sauce. Be careful with Bragg's, because it is very salty.

Always use aluminum free baking powder

Use ghee or extra virgin olive oil, rather than butters and margarines. Ghee is made by simmering unsalted butter in a large pot, or slow cooking in a cast iron skillet in an oven until all of the water has boiled off and the milk solids have settled to the bottom. The cooked and clarified butter is then spooned off to avoid disturbing the milk solids on the bottom of the pan. Unlike butter, ghee can be stored for extended periods without refrigeration, provided it is kept in an or view my video at this link: http://www.youtube.com/watchtv=DVJaqaf7BoE

Avoid soy: that includes soy milk, tofu, etc. There is much controversy over the use of soy. In Asian countries, they only use soy that has been fermented. In America, our soy milk and flours are made from raw soy beans. There are questions about whether the raw soy beans have toxins that the fermented do not. So, when in question, I say avoid it.

Yeast is fed by sugar, so in the early stages you really need to avoid sugar and sweeteners except for stevia. However, when you can add some sweeteners back in to your diet use raw honey, stevia

(sauté NuStevia Powder or SweetLeaf Liquid) or sucanat, which is raw cane syrup that has been dehydrated with all of the minerals intact. Never use white sugar, corn syrup, or regular brown sugar.

Also, because yeast is fed by sugar, should watch the amount of carbs that you consume. Ask your doctor what your target carb intake should be. Usually you need to stay below 80 carbs per day. And, if you are a smaller framed person, you may need to cut that back to even 35-50 carbs per day. Again, ask your doctor what is best for you.

Try to stick with Organic everything!!! It is a little more expensive, but isn't your health worth it in the long run.

Use extra virgin olive oil as your primary cooking oil. If it calls for olive oil, it means extra virgin olive oil made by the cold pressed process. The bottle will say, "Cold Pressed" on the label. If it doesn't say it, don't buy it.

Use safflower oil, coconut oil, walnut oil, almond oil, sesame oil, and grape seed oil sparingly. Avoid all other oils, especially canola. Also look for oils that are cold pressed. That means that no chemicals were used in the process of extracting the oil.

If a recipe calls for milk, use almond, rice or coconut milk. In general, you should avoid dairy when you are on a yeast free diet. That includes milk, cream, sour cream, yogurt, ice cream, cheese, etc…

I have recently found a great substitute for cream. It is called MimicCreme and is made from almonds and cashews. It works very well in recipes. Just be sure that you don't have a problem with nuts.

Corn and corn products can be an allergen for many people. If it causes you problems then avoid it.

Handy breading alternatives for coatings on meat and veggies are corn tortilla chip crumbs crisp rice or corn cereal crumbs, and yeast free rice crackers. Any of these items can be whirled in a blender or food processor to make a quick breading.

Never use refined flour of any kind, especially wheat. Most people with food allergies have problems with wheat. I have my own grain mill, a Whisper Mill, and make my own freshly ground flour from wheat, rice, oat, millet, amaranth, quinoa and legumes. When I use my freshly ground wheat in recipes, I don't have a problem. But again, if your doctor says no, then don't use it.

Always wash produce. There are molds on all fruit and veggies that can not be seen with the naked eye. Use the recipe provided in the Tips & Tricks chapter to make an excellent wash.

Avoid all fermented foods and food containing vinegar. This includes ketchup, mustard, pickles, soy sauce, alcohol, etc…

Read all food labels very carefully. Use the Cooking What's Left Shopping Guide when you go to the store. It will help you make wise choices.

Legal Noodles would be noodles made with spelt, rice, corn, etc. It does not mean basic white refined noodles. They have no nutritional value.

Avoid citric acid, especially in canned goods.

When buying seafood, always look for wild caught, not farm raised. And of course, fish is a much better choice than shellfish.

Never use quick cooking white rice. Stick with healthy brown rice's and rice's that are long cooking.

Egg Substitutes - One egg equals any of the following:

  1 Tb flaxseed - ground in coffee mill or blender

  1 Tb gelatin or fruit pectin

Yogurt, mashed bananas, applesauce, pumpkin, or other pureed fruit or vegetables are good replacements for eggs in muffins or cakes

To replace eggs in casseroles, burgers, or loaves try mashed vegetables, tahini (sesame seed butter, if allowed), nut butters (if allowed), or rolled oats.

Bob's Red Mill Egg Replacer (One of my personal favorite!)

Cooking & Baking with Alternative Whole Grains

Grain	Flavor	Breading	Thickening	Baking
Amaranth	Mild and Nutty	Excellent	Fair	Substitute for 25% of total flour and use another grain, such as rice or oat, to make up the difference
Arrowroot	Flavorless	Good	Excellent, use as you would cornstarch	Substitute for 25% of total flour and use another grain, such as rice or oat, to make up the difference
Brown Rice Flour	Mild	Not Good	Satisfactory, but will take more to thicken than regular flour	Excellent for cookies, pie crusts. To use in cakes add ground nuts to moisten. 7/8 cup rice flour = 1 cup wheat flour
Buckwheat Flour, White	Mild and Mellow	Excellent	Not Good	Excellent for cookies, pie crusts. To use in cakes add ground nuts to moisten.
Garbanzo Bean Flour	Mild	Not Good	Excellent, especially in savory dishes	Excellent. Use 25% with other flours or 50% with ground nuts

Grain	Flavor	Breading	Thickening	Baking
Nut & Seed Flours	Nutty and Rich	Fair	Not Good	Excellent. Use 25% with other flours.
Oat Flour	Mild	Good	Very Good	Excellent for cookies, pie crusts. Can be used for 100% of flour substitution or in combination with another flour.
Potato Flour	Bland & "Potatoey"	Not Good	Good, but does lend a taste of potatoes	Combines well with rice four. 1/2 to 5/8 cup potato flour = 1 cup wheat flour
Potato Starch	Bland	Good	Not Good	Suitable as a portion of the flour for cakes, but needs eggs, baking powder or some other leavening agent.

What To Eat The First Three Weeks

(According to Author of "The Yeast Connection," William G. Crook, M.D. & Dr. Norman Fried)

Foods You Can Eat Freely

<u>Low Carbohydrate Vegetables</u>: These vegetables contain lots of fiber and wonderful essential nutrients. They are relatively low in carbohydrates and calories. You can eat them fresh or frozen, cooked or raw.

- ✓ *Asparagus*
- ✓ *Beet Greens*
- ✓ *Bell Peppers*
- ✓ *Broccoli*
- ✓ *Brussels Sprouts*
- ✓ *Collard Greens*
- ✓ *Daikon*
- ✓ *Dandelion*
- ✓ *Eggplant*
- ✓ *Cabbage*
- ✓ *Carrots*
- ✓ *Cauliflower*
- ✓ *Kale*
- ✓ *Kohlrabi*
- ✓ *Leeks*
- ✓ *Lettuce (All Varieties)*
- ✓ *Mustard Greens*
- ✓ *Okra*
- ✓ *Onions*
- ✓ *Parsley*
- ✓ *Parsnips*
- ✓ *Celery*
- ✓ *Endive*
- ✓ *Garlic*
- ✓ *Radishes*
- ✓ *Rutabaga*
- ✓ *Shallots*
- ✓ *Snow Peas*
- ✓ *Soybeans*
- ✓ *Spinach*
- ✓ *String Beans*
- ✓ *Swiss Chard*
- ✓ *Tomatoes, Fresh*
- ✓ *Turnips*

Meat, Seafood, Eggs and Other Food: Try to always use natural, organic meats and poultry. Look for wild seafood, not farm raised. Avoid nitrates.

- ✓ Beef, Lean Cuts
- ✓ Chicken
- ✓
- ✓ Cod
- ✓ Lamb
- ✓ Mackerel
- ✓ Grouper Other Fresh or Frozen Fish
- ✓ Pork, Lean Cuts
- ✓ Salmon
- ✓ Shellfish: Shrimp, Lobster, Crab
- ✓ Tuna
- ✓ Turkey
- ✓ Veal
- ✓ Wild Game
- ✓ Free Range Eggs

Nuts, Seeds and Oils (unprocessed): Raw nuts and seeds are best. Oils should be cold pressed. Always read labels for hidden ingredients.

- ✓ Almonds
- ✓ Brazil Nuts
- ✓ Cashews
- ✓ Filberts
- ✓ Flaxseeds
- ✓ Pecans
- ✓ Pumpkin Seeds
- ✓ Sunflower Seeds
- ✓ Chia Seeds
- ✓ Sardines
- ✓ Ghee
- ✓ Oils, cold-pressed and unrefined
- ✓ Olive Oil
- ✓ Coconut Oil
- ✓ Safflower Oil
- ✓ Walnut Oil

Foods You Can Eat Cautiously

Higher Carbohydrate Vegetables:

- ✓ Artichoke
- ✓ Avocado
- ✓ Beans, Peas & other Legumes
- ✓ Celery Root
- ✓ Fennel
- ✓ Beets
- ✓ Boniata (white sweet potato)
- ✓ Breadfruit
- ✓ Winter, Acorn or Butternut Squash

Dairy Products: Eat these sparingly since many people have food sensitivities to dairy products. If your symptoms persist, eliminate the completely.

- ✓ Cream Cheese
- ✓ Sour Cream
- ✓ Yogurt
- ✓ Hard Cheeses

Whole Grains & Grain Alternatives: Eat these sparingly since some people have food sensitivities to grains. if your symptoms persist, eliminate them completely.

- ✓ Barley
- ✓ Corn
- ✓ Kamut
- ✓ Millet
- ✓ Oats
- ✓ Brown Rice
- ✓ Spelt
- ✓ Teff
- ✓ Whole Wheat
- ✓ Amaranth
- ✓ Buckwheat
- ✓ Quinoa

Breads, Biscuits & Muffins: All breads, biscuits, muffins, pancakes, waffles, and crackers should be made with baking powder or baking soda as a leavening agent rather than yeast.

Foods You Must Avoid Completely

Sugar and Foods Containing Sugar: Avoid sugar and other quick-acting carbohydrates, including sucrose, fructose, maltose, lactose, glycogen, glucose, mannitol, sorbitol, galactose, monosaccharides and polysaccharides. Also avoid honey, molasses, maple sugar, date sugar and turbinado sugar.

Packaged and Processed Foods: Canned, bottled, boxed and other packaged and processed foods usually contain refined sugar products and other hidden ingredients. You'll not only need to avoid these sugar-containing foods in the early weeks of your diet, but you'll probably need to avoid them indefinitely.

Foods Containing Yeast: Avoid yeast-containing foods for at least the first 10 days of your diet. Here's a list of foods that contain yeasts or molds:

Breads, pastries and other raised-bakery goods.

Cheeses: all cheeses. Moldy cheeses, such as Roquefort, are the worst.

Condiments, sauces and vinegar-containing foods: mustard, barbecue, chili, shrimp and soy sauces; pickles, pickled vegetables, relishes, green olives, sauerkraut, horseradish, mincemeat and tamari.

Vinegar and all kinds of vinegar-containing foods, such as mayonnaise and salad dressing. (Freshly squeezed lemon juice may be used as a substitute for vinegar in salad dressings prepared with unprocessed vegetable oil).

Malt products: malted milk drinks, cereals and candy. (Malt is a sprouted grain that is kiln-dried and used in the preparation of man processed foods and beverages).

Processed and smoked meats: pickled and smoked meats and fish, including bacon, ham, sausages, hot dogs, corned beef, pastrami and pickled tongue.

Edible fungi: all types of mushrooms, morels and truffles.

Melons: watermelon, honeydew and, especially, cantaloupe.

Dried and candied fruits: raisins, apricots, dates, prunes, figs and pineapple.

Leftovers: molds grow in leftover food unless it's properly refrigerated. Freezing is better.

What To Drink

What To Drink Freely

Water: You should drink at least eight glasses of water a day. Yet, ordinary tap water may be contaminated with lead, bacteria or parasites. So, try to use a water filter or purchase filtered water preferably in glass bottles.

Coffee & Teas: These popular beverages, including the health food teas, are prepared from plant products. Although these products are subject to mold contamination, most people seem to tolerate them. Teas of various kinds, including taheebo (Pau d'Arco), have been reported to have therapeutic value.

If you can't get along without your coffee, limit your intake to one or two cups a day. Drink it plain or sweetened with stevia. Do not use artificial sweeteners.

Drinks To Avoid

Fruit Juices: These popular beverages are a big "no-no," even more so than eating fresh fruit. Most fruit juices, including frozen, bottled or canned, are prepared from fruits that have been allowed to stand in bins, barrels and other containers for periods ranging from an hour to several days or weeks. Although juice processors discard fruits that are obviously spoiled by mold, most fruits used for juice contain some level of mold.

Alcoholic Beverages: Wines, beers and other alcoholic beverages contain high levels of yeast contamination, so if you're allergic to yeast, you'll need to avoid them. You should stay away from alcoholic beverages for another reason: they contain large amounts of quick-acting carbohydrates. If you drink these beverages, you will be feeding your yeast.

Diet Drinks: These beverages possess no nutritional value. Moreover, they're usually sweetened with aspartame (Nutrasweet), which causes adverse reactions in many people. They also may contain caffeine, food coloring, phosphates and other ingredients that many individuals can't tolerate. However, since diet drinks do not contain mold, some people with candida-related problems can tolerate them. If you drink them, use them sparingly. The Four Stage Process To Controlling

Your Symptoms

Four Stages In Controlling Your Symptoms

A Yeast Fighting diet should have four distinct stages. For best results, it should be followed in order from elimination to maintenance:

Elimination: The elimination of sugar and yeast containing foods

Challenge: Reintroduce some foods you've eliminated and check reactions

Reassessment: Explore food allergies and sensitivities

Maintenance: Eat those foods that work for you

The Steps

1. Elimination

In the first stage, you'll eliminate foods that feed yeast organisms and encourage overgrowth. These include sugar, yeast, mold, starches and fermented foods.

The Elimination Stage usually needs to last for 2 to 4 weeks, depending on how long it takes your major symptoms to subside. The simplest approach is to focus on eating fresh meats, vegetables, raw nuts and seeds, unprocessed oils, water and herb tea.

Eating other foods during this stage may slow the process of clearing yeast and toxins from your body. It may also be more difficult to notice a direct link between foods and symptoms. You may find that some of these don't cause you trouble at all. Feel free to experiment. Just tune in to your body's signals and document what happens.

As you eliminate yeast-feeding food from your diet and incorporate supplements or other medication, you may experience "die-off." This is actually a great sign that you're on the right track!

2. Challenge

You are ready for the challenge stage when you have experienced some relief and begun to control your yeast overgrowth. Now you're ready to reintroduce or "challenge" some of the foods you avoided in Stage 1.

Continue following the food plan from the elimination stage. Add one portion of one new food a day and notice any reactions or symptoms your body experiences in response to the new food. If you notice a reaction, give yourself at least one day without symptoms before introducing another new food. If you don't notice a reaction, continue another new food per day and observe your body's response.

When reintroducing foods, start with foods containing only one ingredient. Because if you experience a reaction to bread, the culprit could be yeast, wheat, eggs, or sugar. It could be difficult to pinpoint which food is causing you discomfort. It would be better to try cooked wheat berries one day, eggs on another day and so on. Next, you may want to reintroduce fruit. Try only one type of fruit initially and watch for your body's response. Then move on to another food. For best results, don't eat sugar until your body has been clear of symptoms for several months.

Record the foods you eat each day and body symptoms and sensations linked to eating those foods. When you have a good list of foods that your body seems to tolerate and not tolerate, it's time to move to Stage 3, Reassessment.

3. Reassessment

If you are feeling much better, you may choose to go on to Maintenance. But, maybe you still have quite a few symptoms. At this point, you might have accumulated a long list of foods that set you off. Now it's time for the reassessment phase.

Avoid the foods on your list for at least two weeks. Also avoid any food or beverage you consume over once a week. Many times the foods that we crave and eat often are the very foods that cause us problems. Track your normal week's intake and note which foods appear on the chart frequently. Some people need 3-4 weeks to purge the toxins from a particular food to notice a distinct change. If you don't detect a noticeable difference in symptoms, continue this process for a few more weeks.

Once you do feel better, gradually integrate each food back into your diet. Add only one new item at a time. Allow at least a day or two between each addition to help you clearly identify any symptoms that might be caused by that particular food. Make sure you track in detail your food and symptoms as you do these experiments.

If you don't notice any symptoms, wait another four to seven days before eating that particular food again. This rotation of foods helps you detect hidden sensitivities. If you notice symptoms, avoid that food. You may want to discuss allergy treatments with your health care professional. This may allow you to eat a particular food without problems. You may, however, need to avoid it on a regular basis.

By the end of reassessment, you will have developed a list of foods you can and cannot tolerate. It's now time to move to Maintenance.

4. Maintenance

Congratulations! You may not be all the way back to where you want to be, but you have faced a challenge -- and you've acquired valuable knowledge about yourself and your body. Now you can loosen up a bit. You now know what to watch for and how to return to a more restricted food plan any time you run into trouble. And remember, diet is only one part of the program.

Don't forget other ways to care for yourself. Most importantly, notice and trust your intuition. Humans have great instincts about what works for them and what doesn't. Remember, even respected professionals don't know everything. Don't let anyone convince you that you don't know what you're talking about. You alone are the "expert" on yourself and your body. Take advantage of available resources, and talk to others, but don't devalue your own instincts.

Chapter 2

Appetizers, Starters & Snacks

Stage Number 1

Better Than Crackers

This simple recipe can be made the way it instructs, or add salt once you have brushed with ghee for a savory snack. For a sweet snack, add stevia to the melted ghee and then dust with cinnamon. Or, use sucanat with honey and cinnamon to dust the tortillas (Stage 2).

Ingredients

- ✓ 4 organic corn tortillas
- ✓ 1/2 cup ghee, melted

Directions

Brush both sides of tortillas with ghee. Lay flat on baking sheets and place in a cold oven. Heat oven to 375° and then cut off. Leave tortillas in oven until cool. Do not open the door.

Cooking Tips

The tortillas can be cut into wedges before baking.

Stage Number 1

Crispy Tortilla Threads

My family loves these. They are delicious by themselves or floating on top of soup or in a taco or fajita salad. The options are endless.

Ingredients

- ✓ Vegetable oil, for frying
- ✓ 4 white corn tortillas, cut into thin strips
- ✓ Salt

Directions

In a medium saucepan heat enough vegetable oil to come 2-inches up the sides of the pan to 350° degrees.

Stack the tortillas and with a large very sharp knife slice into long thin strips. The strips from the center of the tortillas can be too long, so I will cut them in half.

When hot, add half of the tortilla threads and cook until golden brown, 2 to 3 minutes. Remove with a slotted spoon and transfer to a paper-lined plate to drain.

Season with salt, to taste.

Stage Number 1

Egg Rolls Without The Roll

Sometimes I get a craving for egg rolls. So, I decided why not just create a filling that was great all by itself. Another option is to use a rice paper wrapper. Make sure you check the ingredients. A great accompaniment is wasabi powder mixed with a little water. Enjoy!

Ingredients

- ✓ 1/2 lb ground beef
- ✓ 1 lb. pkg. coleslaw mix (grated cabbage and carrots)
- ✓ 1/2 tsp black pepper
- ✓ 1 tsp chopped garlic
- ✓ 1/2 tsp ground ginger
- ✓ 2 tbs Bragg's Amino Acids
- ✓ 1 egg - beaten

Directions

Brown beef in skillet and drain off fat.

Add coleslaw mix, black pepper, garlic, and ginger to skillet. Stir-fry until all is tender. Drain and any liquid from pan.

Stir in Bragg's.

Stage Number 1

Eggplant Balls

Ingredients

- ✓ 4 medium eggplants
- ✓ 2 tbs. freshly milled whole grain flour 1 large egg
- ✓ 1/2 tsp white pepper
- ✓ 1 small Italian pepper
- ✓ 1 cup oil
- ✓ salt to taste

Directions

Peel eggplants, quarter and boil in salted water until tender.

Combine all ingredients except oil in food processor until smooth paste is formed.

Heat oil in heavy pot and drop in eggplant paste a spoonful at a time. Fry until golden.

Salt to taste. Drain on paper towels.

Stage Number 1

Falafel

Ingredients

- ✓ 2 cups dried chickpeas, picked through and rinsed
- ✓ 1 tsp baking powder
- ✓ 1 small onion, coarsely chopped
- ✓ 6 garlic cloves, smashed
- ✓ 1 Tbs cumin seeds, toasted and ground
- ✓ 1 Tbs coriander seeds, toasted and ground
- ✓ 1/4 tsp red pepper flakes
- ✓ 2 handfuls fresh flat-leaf parsley, leaves coarsely chopped
- ✓ 1 handful fresh cilantro, leaves coarsely chopped
- ✓ Kosher salt and freshly ground black pepper
- ✓ Vegetable oil, for frying

Directions

Put the dried chickpeas in a large bowl and add cool water to cover by 2 inches. Soak the beans in the refrigerator for at least 18 hours or up to 24; the chickpeas will swell to triple their original size.

Drain and rinse thoroughly.

Put the soaked chickpeas in a food processor and pulse to coarsely grind, not until smooth but with no whole chickpeas remaining either.

Add the baking powder, onion, garlic, spices, and herbs; process until the mixture is pureed; scraping down the sides of the bowl as needed. Taste and season with salt and pepper.

Transfer to a bowl and refrigerate while heating the oil, this should take about 15 minutes. Pour 3-inches of the oil in a deep fryer or deep heavy pot and heat to 375° degrees F.

Roll the falafel mixture into ping-pong size balls. (Alternatively, use an ice cream scoop.) Carefully slip a few at a time into the hot oil, making sure they don't stick to the bottom. Fry until the chickpea fritters are a crusty dark brown on all sides, turning as needed, about 5 minutes per batch.

Remove the falafels with a slotted spoon and drain on a platter lined with paper towels.

Stage Number 1

Rosemary Lemon Popcorn

This simple recipe is great when you have the munchies or for a special treat on movie night.

Ingredients

- ✓ 1 cup popcorn
- ✓ 3 Tbs extra-virgin olive oil
- ✓ 3 Tbs melted ghee
- ✓ 1 Tbs finely chopped rosemary leaves
- ✓ 2 tsp salt
- ✓ freshly ground black pepper
- ✓ 1 Tbs grated lemon zest

Directions

Heat the popcorn and oil in a 1-gallon, heavy bottomed pot over medium-high heat. When the popcorn starts to pop, cover the pot tightly and continue to cook until all the popcorn pops, about 2 to 3 minutes, shaking the pot occasionally.

Pour the popcorn into a large bowl.

In a medium sauté pan over medium-high heat, melt the ghee. Remove the pan from the heat. Add the rosemary to the ghee and pour the mixture over the popcorn. Toss well. Add the salt, pepper and lemon zest. Toss well.

Chapter 3

Beverages

Stage Number 1

Fresh Tomato Juice

This simple recipe can be made the way it instructs, or add salt once you have brushed with ghee for a savory snack. For a sweet snack, add stevia to the melted ghee and then dust with cinnamon. Or, use sucanat with honey and cinnamon to dust the tortillas (Stage 2).

Ingredients

- ✓ 5 medium very ripe tomatoes, halved
- ✓ salt
- ✓ freshly ground black pepper
- ✓ 1/2 lemon, juiced

Directions

Place the halved tomatoes, skin side down in a large nonstick skillet. Drizzle with a tablespoon of water. Cover and cook over medium heat for 30 minutes. Check occasionally to make sure that there is liquid in the pan, add a little water at a time.

Pour the tomatoes and juice into a sieve placed over a large bowl. Mash the tomatoes with a wooden spoon to get all the pulp through the sieve without seeds and skin.

Add salt and pepper to taste and a little lemon juice. Chill and serve over ice.

Serves 2

Stage Number 1

Sparkling Lemonade

This is one of mine and my husbands favorite drinks. Very Refreshing!

Ingredients

- ✓ 1 lemon
- ✓ 5-10 drops clear liquid stevia
- ✓ club soda or sparkling mineral water

Directions

Cut the lemon in half. Squeeze 1/2 of the lemon into a glass of ice. Add the liquid stevia to the glass and then fill to the top with club soda.

Serves 2

Chapter 4

Breads

Stage Number 1

Applesauce Bread

Ingredients

- ✓ 1/2 cup ghee
- ✓ 1/4 cup sucanat
- ✓ 2 1/4 cups freshly ground flour (wheat, rice, oat, millet or a mixture)
- ✓ 1 tsp baking powder
- ✓ 1 tsp baking soda
- ✓ 1/2 tsp salt
- ✓ 1 tsp ground cinnamon
- ✓ tsp allspice
- ✓ 1 tsp vanilla
- ✓ 1 cup applesauce, organic unsweetened
- ✓ 2 large eggs

Directions

Preheat the oven to 350 degrees F. Grease and flour an 8 by 4 by 3-inch loaf pan.

Cream the butter and sucanat. Add the remaining ingredients. Mix well until blended. Pour into the loaf pan.

Bake for 45 to 55 minutes or until center tests done.

Preparation time: 10 minutes

Cooking time: 65 minutes

Stage Number 2

Baking Mix

Ingredients

- ✓ 8 cups freshly milled whole grain flour
- ✓ 5 tbs baking powder
- ✓ 1 tb salt
- ✓ 1-2 cups dry milk powder, only if allowed
- ✓ 1 1/2 cups ghee

Directions

Combine dry ingredients well in a large bowl. Cut in oil or butter with fingers or a food processor to make fine crumbs. Store in a tightly covered container in the refrigerator.

Preparation time: 10 minutes

Cooking Tips

Milk powder may be omitted in case of milk allergies.

Recipe can be doubled. You can also substitute different grains for the wheat. Use cornmeal, oat, rye, brown rice, or other whole grain flour. Play around and make your own.

Stage Number 2

Baking Mix Biscuits

Ingredients

- ✓ 3 cups Baking Mix
- ✓ 2/3 cup legal milk or water
- ✓ Optional: herbs or spices

Directions

Stir liquid into Mix just until moistened.

Knead briefly on floured surface. Roll or pat out to 1/2 inch thick and cut into biscuits.

Bake at 400° for 10 minutes.

Stage Number 2

Baking Mix Cornbread

Ingredients

- ✓ 1 1/2 cups Baking Mix
- ✓ 3/4 cup cornmeal
- ✓ 1 tb honey, optional
- ✓ 1 egg
- ✓ 1 cup liquid (could use rice milk, broth, tomato juice, etc.)

Directions

Combine mix, cornmeal and honey. Add milk and egg, beaten together.

Stir just until moistened and pour into an 8" square pan or hot greased cast iron skillet.

Bake at 400° for 25 to 30 minutes.

Stage Number 2

Baking Mix Mexican Cornbread

Ingredients

- ✓ 1 1/2 cups Baking Mix
- ✓ 3/4 cup cornmeal
- ✓ 1 tb honey, optional
- ✓ 1 egg
- ✓ 1/2 cup liquid (could use rice milk, broth, tomato juice, etc.)
- ✓ 1/2 cup salsa, vinegar-free
- ✓ 1 cup whole corn kernels, thawed, drained or cut from the cob
- ✓ 1 can diced green chilies

Directions

Combine mix, cornmeal and honey. Add liquids and egg, beaten together.

Stir just until moistened. Add the corn and green chilies and mix well. Pour into an 8" square pan or hot greased cast iron skillet.

Bake at 400° for 25 to 30 minutes.

Stage Number 2

Baking Mix Muffins

Ingredients

- ✓ 3 cups baking mix
- ✓ 3-4 tbs Sucanat or Honey, if allowed
- ✓ 1 cup almond or nut milk
- ✓ 1 egg
- ✓ 3-4 tbs ghee or oil
- ✓ 1 cup fruit, if allowed
- ✓ 1 tb cinnamon

Directions

Beat sweetener, liquid, ghee and egg together and stir into Mix just until moistened. Fold in optional fruit and spices, if used.

Fill 12 greased muffin cups and bake at 400° for 20 minutes.

Stage Number 2

Banana Bread

Ingredients

- ✓ 1 3/4 cups freshly milled whole grain flour
- ✓ 1 tsp cinnamon
- ✓ 2 tsp baking powder
- ✓ 1/2 tsp soda
- ✓ 1/4 tsp salt
- ✓ 1/4 cup oil
- ✓ 1/4 cup honey
- ✓ 3/4 cup yogurt, rice or soy based unless you can tolerate dairy
- ✓ 1 egg
- ✓ 1 cup banana (about 2-3)

Directions

Process the banana in a blender with the oil and egg until well blended. Stir in with the other liquid ingredients.

Combine the dry ingredients. Slowly add the liquids and mix well. Pour into a greased loaf pan.

Bake at 350° for 45-50 minutes. Cool 10 minutes.

Stage Number 2

Old Fashioned Corn Cakes

Ingredients

- ✓ 1 tsp salt
- ✓ 2 cups boiling water
- ✓ 1 1/4 cups white cornmeal
- ✓ Vegetable oil alone or add bacon drippings (only use a small amount and it should come from nitrate free bacon), enough to fill skillet 1-inch deep

Directions

Add the salt to the boiling water; gradually sift in the cornmeal. Stir to combine. Cool the mixture in the refrigerator for 20 minutes.

Shape into balls and then flatten to form patties about 2-inches across.

Heat the vegetable oil or bacon drippings in a skillet. Fry patties until golden brown, about 5 minutes. Turn once. Drain and serve hot.

Cooking Tips

Coat hands with oil to prevent batter from sticking when shaping the balls.

Chapter 5

Chowders, Soups & Stews

Stage Number 1

Basic UnCanned Condensed Soup

Ingredients

- ✓ 3 tbs ghee
- ✓ 3 tbs whole grain flour
- ✓ 1/4 tsp salt
- ✓ dash pepper
- ✓ 1 1/4 cups liquid (legal milk or stock)

Directions

Melt butter in saucepan. Stir in flour and seasonings. Cook over medium heat until bubbly. Add liquid slowly, stirring with wire whisk to prevent lumps. Cook until thick.

Stage Number 1

Broccoli Soup

For a Cream of Broccoli Soup, simply take a 1/3 cup of dry white beans (lima, northern) and pulse in a blender until it looks like flour. Add this flour into a small amount of the soup until it is well mixed. Then stir the bean mixture into the pot of soup. Yummy!

Ingredients

- ✓ 2 Tbs ghee
- ✓ 1 head broccoli, chopped
- ✓ 4 cups chicken stock
- ✓ salt
- ✓ pepper

Directions

Place a large saucepan over low heat. Add the ghee or oil and stir until just melted. Add the broccoli and sauté until tender, about 7 minutes.

Add the chicken stock and bring to a boil. Lower the heat and simmer for 20 minutes.

Use a hand blender and carefully use to puree the soup to the consistency that you like. If you use a blender, be very careful. Hot liquids added to a blender can explode. This is why I prefer the hand blender

Add the salt and pepper to taste.

Serve immediately. You can garnish with a sprinkling of fresh chives.

Serves 6

Preparation time: 10 minutes Cooking time: 30 minutes Ready in: 40 minutes

Stage Number 1

Caramelized Roasted Fennel Soup

Ingredients

- ✓ 3 bulbs fennel, sliced 1/4 thick
- ✓ 1 medium onion, sliced 1/4 inch thick
- ✓ 3 cloves garlic
- ✓ extra virgin olive oil
- ✓ salt
- ✓ freshly ground black pepper
- ✓ 3 cups chicken broth
- ✓ 1/2 cup legal milk
- ✓ chopped fresh chives for garnish

Directions

Preheat the oven to 375°.

Place the fennel, onion and garlic on a baking pan. Drizzle with Olive Oil and season with salt and pepper. Roast in the oven for 45 minutes, or until the vegetables are caramelized and soft.

Scrape all the vegetables into a blender or food processor. Add the chicken broth and puree until smooth. Adjust with more broth, if necessary.

Strain into a soup pot and add the milk. Heat over medium until hot. Adjust seasonings with additional salt and pepper.

Ladle into bowls and garnish with chives.

Stage Number 1

Corn & Crab Chowder

Ingredients

- ✓ 1 Tb olive oil
- ✓ 1 Tb ghee
- ✓ 2 medium potatoes, diced
- ✓ 1 stalk celery, chopped or
- ✓ 1 tsp celery seed
- ✓ 1 medium onion, chopped
- ✓ 1 small red pepper, seeded and chopped
- ✓ 1 bay leaf, fresh or dried
- ✓ freshly ground black pepper
- ✓ salt
- ✓ 1 Tbs Seafood Seasoning
- ✓ 3 Tbs legal whole grain flour
- ✓ 2 cups chicken or seafood broth
- ✓ 1 quart legal milk
- ✓ 2 cans corn kernels, canned & drained or
- ✓ 1 bag frozen corn kernels
- ✓ 8 oz cooked lump crab meat, canned or fresh

Directions

Heat a large saucepan over medium high heat. Add oil and ghee.

Add the chopped vegetables to the pot: potatoes, celery, onion, and red pepper.

Add bay leaf to the pot. Season vegetables with salt and pepper and seafood seasoning.

Sauté vegetables for 5 minutes, then sprinkle in the flour. Cook the flour for 2 minutes, stirring constantly.

Slowly stir in the broth and mix well.

Stir in the milk and mix well. Bring soup up to a boil.

Add the corn and the crab meat and simmer soup 5 minutes.

Adjust the soup seasonings. Remove bay leaf.

Ladle into bowls and serve with fresh chives sprinkled on top.

Serves 4

Preparation time: 10 minutes Cooking time: 20 minutes

Stage Number 1

Fresh & Quick Tomato Soup

Ingredients

- ✓ 6 - 8 ripe tomatoes
- ✓ 2 tbs olive oil
- ✓ 1 onion, thinly sliced
- ✓ 2 cloves garlic, smashed
- ✓ salt
- ✓ ground black pepper
- ✓ 1 sprig fresh basil leaves removed from stem and chopped fine

Directions

Coarsely chop the tomatoes and set aside.

Heat a small stockpot on medium and add the olive oil and onion. Cook the onion until translucent, about 10 minutes, then add the garlic cloves and continue caramelizing the onion for another 10 min.

Add the tomatoes and bring just to a boil. Season with salt and pepper, to taste.

Reduce the heat and add the basil. Simmer for about 2 minutes. Remove the pot from the heat.

Puree with a hand blender until desired consistency. Adjust the seasoning.

Serves 4

Preparation time: 10 minutes Cooking time: 30 minutes Ready in: 40 minutes

Stage Number 1

Gumbo

Ingredients

- ✓ 3 large boneless skinless chicken breast halves
- ✓ Salt and pepper
- ✓ 1/4 cup olive oil
- ✓ 1 pound smoked sausage, nitrate-free, cut into 1/4-inch slices (turkey sausage is a good option)
- ✓ 1/2 cup legal whole grain flour
- ✓ 5 Tbs ghee
- ✓ 1 large onion, chopped
- ✓ 8 cloves garlic, minced
- ✓ 1 green bell pepper, seeded and chopped
- ✓ 3 stalks celery, chopped
- ✓ 2 Tb Bragg's Amino Acids
- ✓ 1/4 cup flat leaf parsley, stems and leaves, coarsely chopped, plus chopped leaves for garnish
- ✓ 4 cups beef broth
- ✓ 1 14 oz can stewed tomatoes with juice
- ✓ 2 cups frozen sliced okra
- ✓ 4 green onions, sliced, white and green parts
- ✓ 1/2 lb. small shrimp, peeled, deveined and cooked

Directions

Season the chicken with salt and pepper. Heat the oil in a heavy bottomed Dutch oven over medium-high heat. Cook the chicken until browned on both sides and remove. Add the sausage and cook until browned, then remove.

Sprinkle the flour over the oil, add 2 tablespoons of ghee and cook over medium heat, stirring constantly, until brown, about 10 minutes. Congratulations, you have just made a roux. Let the roux cool.

Return the Dutch oven to low heat and melt the remaining 3 tablespoons ghee. Add the onion, garlic, green pepper and celery and cook for 10 minutes. Add Bragg's, salt and pepper, to taste and the parsley. Cook, while stirring frequently, for 10 minutes.

Add 4 cups of beef stock, whisking constantly.

Add the chicken and sausage. Bring to a boil, then reduce the heat, cover, and simmer for 45 minutes.

Add tomatoes and okra. Cover and simmer for 1 hour.

Just before serving add the green onions, shrimp and chopped parsley.

Serves 8

Stage Number 1

Irish Stew

Ingredients

- ✓ 1 1/2 lb. Beef Cubes
- ✓ 1/2 tsp Real Salt
- ✓ 1/2 tsp Ground Black Pepper
- ✓ 1/2 tsp Paprika
- ✓ 1 tsp Onion Powder
- ✓ 1/2 tsp Seasoning Salt
- ✓ 1 cup Oat Flour
- ✓ 3 Tbs. Olive Oi
- ✓ 1 bag Frozen Organic Mixed Veggies
- ✓ 1/2 cup Cold Water

Directions

Mix flour, salt, pepper, paprika and seasoning salt together in a bowl or zip-lock type bag. Add beef cubes and shake to dust the beef with the flour mixture.

Brown in oil over Med/High heat.

Add water to the pan until the meat is just covered. Simmer covered 1-2 hours adding water if needed.

Slowly mix 2 Tb flour with 1/2 cup cold water. Stir into soup. If the soup is not thick enough repeat with another 2 Tb flour and 1/2 cup cold water.

Once thick and hot add the frozen vegetables. Heat through.

Serves 4

Stage Number 1

Large Batch Condensed Cream of Celery Soup

You can use 1 cup of this mixture as a healthy replacement for Traditional Canned Cream Soups.

Ingredients

- ✓ 1 1/4 cup ghee
- ✓ 1 1/4 cup legal whole grain flour
- ✓ 1 1/2 cups finely chopped celery
- ✓ 1 tsp onion powder
- ✓ 1/2 Tbs. salt
- ✓ 1/4 tsp pepper
- ✓ 5-6 cups chicken stock or
- ✓ 5-6 cups legal milk

Directions

Melt butter in saucepan. Sauté celery. Stir in flour and seasonings. Cook over medium heat until slightly brown.

Add liquid slowly, stirring with wire whisk to prevent lumps. Cook until thick.

Freeze in 1 cup containers.

Serves 6

Stage Number 1

Large Batch Condensed Cream of Chicken Soup

You can use 1 cup of this mixture as a healthy replacement for Traditional Canned Cream Soups.

Ingredients

- 1 1/4 cup ghee
- 1 1/4 cup legal whole grain flour
- 1 1/2 tsp poultry seasoning
- 1/4 tsp onion powder
- 1 Tbs. salt
- 1/4 tsp pepper
- 5-6 cups chicken stock or
- 5-6 cups plain milk substitute

Directions

Melt butter in saucepan. Stir in flour and seasonings. Cook over medium heat until slightly brown.

Add liquid slowly, stirring with wire whisk to prevent lumps. Add cheese. Cook until thick.

Freeze in 1 cup containers.

Serves 6

Stage Number 1

Quick & Savory Chili

This is one of my families favorites I usually triple or quadruple the recipe and freeze it. The taste just gets better and better!

Ingredients

- ✓ 1 lb. natural ground beef
- ✓ 1 Tbs. onion powder or 1 large onion, chopped
- ✓ 1 clove garlic, crushed
- ✓ 1 small can organic tomato sauce
- ✓ 1 small can organic tomato paste
- ✓ /4 tsp sea salt
- ✓ 1/8 tsp freshly ground pepper
- ✓ 3-4 Tbs. chili powder
- ✓ 1 cup water
- ✓ 1 can undrained, organic kidney beans

Directions

Brown the ground beef and drain. Stir in the remaining ingredients. Cover, Reduce heat and simmer for 30 minutes. Stirring occasionally.

Serves 4

Stage Number 1

Roasted Red Pepper Soup

Ingredients

- ✓ 3 cups vegetable broth
- ✓ 12 roasted red peppers, skins removed
- ✓ 1 medium onion, chopped
- ✓ 2 cloves garlic
- ✓ 1/4 tsp red pepper flakes
- ✓ salt
- ✓ freshly ground black pepper

Directions

In a stockpot, bring the broth to a boil. Add the red peppers, onion, garlic, and pepper flakes. Bring back to a boil, then immediately reduce the heat and simmer for 10 minutes.

Transfer to a blender and blend until smooth. Add salt and pepper to taste.

Serves 6

Stage Number 1

The Best Split Pea Soup

Ingredients

- ✓ 8 slices bacon (about 1/4 pound), nitrate free
- ✓ 1/2 onion, chopped
- ✓ 2 carrots, cut into 1/4-inch dice
- ✓ 1 lb. dried split peas
- ✓ 2 1/2 quarts water (plus additional if necessary)
- ✓ 1 ham bone with meat, nitrate free
- ✓ 1 tsp salt
- ✓ 1 bay leaf

Directions

In a large heavy kettle cook bacon over moderate heat, stirring, until crisp and transfer to paper towels to drain.

Pour off all but about 1/4 cup bacon fat from kettle and cook onions and carrots, stirring, until softened.

Add remaining ingredients and simmer, uncovered, stirring occasionally and adding 1 to 2 cups more water if soup becomes too thick, 2 hours.

Remove kettle from heat and transfer ham bone with a slotted spoon to a cutting board. Discard fat and bones and chop meat.

Return meat to kettle and simmer soup, stirring, until heated through. Discard bay leaf.

Just before serving, crumble bacon and sprinkle over soup.

Stage Number 1

Tortilla Soup

Ingredients

- ✓ 2 Tbs. olive oil
- ✓ 1 cup chopped onions
- ✓ 2 tsp chopped garlic
- ✓ 1 green bell pepper, seeded and chopped
- ✓ 1 1/2 tsp salt
- ✓ 1 1/2 tsp ground cumin
- ✓ 1/2 tsp ground coriander
- ✓ 1 Tbs. tomato paste
- ✓ 6 cups chicken stock
- ✓ 1 lb. boneless, skinless chicken breasts, trimmed and cut into 1/2-inch cubes
- ✓ 1/4 cup chopped fresh cilantro leaves
- ✓ 2 tsp fresh lime juice
- ✓ 2 stale corn tortillas, cut into 1/4-inch-thick strips
- ✓ 1 avocado, peeled, seeded, and chopped, for garnish

Directions

In a Dutch oven or large heavy pot, heat the oil on medium-high heat. Add the onions, garlic, peppers, salt, cumin, and coriander for 5 minutes.

Add the tomato paste and cook, stirring, for 1 minute.

Add the chicken stock and bring to a simmer. Simmer for 20 minutes.

Add the chicken and the corn tortillas and let simmer for 15 minutes.

Add the cilantro and lime juice, and stir well.

Ladle the soup into 4 or 6 serving bowls. Garnish each serving with the diced avocado and crispy tortilla threads.

Serves 4

Stage Number 1

Tuscan White Bean Soup

Ingredients

- ✓ 16 oz bag dried cannelloni beans
- ✓ 6 cups chicken broth
- ✓ extra virgin olive oil
- ✓ 1 Tb ghee
- ✓ 1/2 onion, diced
- ✓ 1 clove garlic, minced
- ✓ 1/2 celery root, peeled and diced
- ✓ 1 stalk celery, diced
- ✓ 1 bunch kale, roughly chopped
- ✓ 1 Tbs. tomato paste
- ✓ salt
- ✓ ground pepper
- ✓ 1 sprig rosemary, chopped or
- ✓ 1 tsp dried rosemary
- ✓ 1 sprig thyme, leaves removed and chopped or
- ✓ 1/2 tsp dried thyme

Directions

Place the dried beans into a large mixing bowl and cover by 3 inches with cold water. Allow to soak overnight at room temperature.

Drain the beans and place into a stockpot. Cover with the chicken broth and bring to a boil. Reduce heat to low and simmer until the beans are tender, about 1 hour.

Place another stockpot on medium heat and add the olive oil, butter, onion, garlic, celery root and celery. Sauté until the vegetables are soft, about 20 minutes. Add the kale and cook for 2 to 3 more minutes, until wilted.

Add the tomato paste and stir to combine. Add the cooked beans, including the broth if the soup has become too thick. Season with salt and pepper. Add more broth if the soup has become too thick. Add the rosemary and thyme.

Ladle into soup bowls and garnish with fresh herbs. Serves 4

Chapter 6

Dessert

Stage Number 1

Hot Toffee In A Mug

Ingredients

- ✓ 1 mug of hot water
- ✓ 1 dropper full of Sweet Leaf Liquid Stevia English Toffee Flavor, or any flavor of your choice

Directions

Add one dropper full of the liquid stevia to a mug of hot water. A delicious, zero calorie, zero carb treat!

Serves 1

Stage Number 1

Cocoa Bark

Coconut oil is an excellent fungal fighter and kills yeast. It will also help to increase your metabolism rate. A piece or 2 of this dark chocolate treat should be a part of your daily routine.

Ingredients

- ✓ 1 cup Hershey's Special Dark Cocoa Powder, unsweetened
- ✓ 1 cup coconut oil, melted
- ✓ 1 teaspoon stevia (NuStevia Pure White Powder or SweetLeaf Liquid), or to taste

Directions

Mix all ingredients together in a bowl and then pour onto a parchment lined baking sheet with sides. Spread the mixture out to a thin uniform layer.

Place in the refrigerator until hardened. Break into bite size pieces. Store in the refrigerator. Coconut oil melts at room temperature.

Yield: About 1 1/2 cups

Stage Number 2

Apple Crisp

Ingredients

- ✓ 4 large baking apples, peeled, sliced **
- ✓ 1/2 teaspoon stevia (NuStevia Powder or SweetLeaf Liquid)
- ✓ 1/2 cup freshly milled whole wheat flour, rice flour, or oat flour
- ✓ 3/4 cup oatmeal
- ✓ 3/4 tsp cinnamon
- ✓ 3/4 tsp nutmeg
- ✓ 1/3 cup ghee
- ✓ ** Granny Smith Apples are low on the glycemic index, so probably they are your best bet!

Directions

Heat the oven to 350° degrees. Spray a baking pan with nonstick cooking spray and place the apples in the pan.

Mix the sucanat, flour, oatmeal, cinnamon, and nutmeg together and place on top of the apple. Drop dots of margarine over the dry mixture. Bake for 25 minutes.

Serves 6

Stage Number 1

Creamy Custard

Ingredients

- ✓ 2 eggs
- ✓ 1/4 teaspoon stevia (NuStevia Powder or SweetLeaf Liquid)
- ✓ 1 tsp vanilla
- ✓ 2/3 cups coconut milk
- ✓ 1/2 tsp nutmeg

Directions

Heat the oven to 325° degrees.

Combine the eggs, stevia, vanilla, and milk in a medium bowl. Beat well and pour into individual custard cups or a baking dish.

Sprinkle nutmeg over the mixture and bake for 35 minutes. The custard is done when a knife inserted in the center of the custard comes out clean.

Serves 4

Stage Number 2

Creamy Eggless Rice Pudding

Ingredients

- ✓   1 1/2 quarts vanilla almond milk
- ✓   1 teaspoon stevia (NuStevia Pure White Powder or SweetLeaf Liquid) for Stage 1
- ✓   1 cup sucanat with honey (optional for Stage 2)
- ✓   1/2 cup basmati rice, white
- ✓   1 tsp vanilla

Directions

Combine the milk, stevia and rice in a heavy saucepan. Bring to a gentle boil over medium heat. Reduce heat to simmer and cook uncovered for 1 hour, stirring occasionally.

Add raisins, increase heat to medium and cook, stirring frequently, until rice has absorbed most of the milk, but not all, and pudding is creamy (about 30 minutes longer).

Remove from pan and stir in the vanilla. When cool, pudding will thicken, but will still be very creamy. Serve warm or well chilled.

Serves 8

Stage Number 2

Instant Rice Pudding with Cinnamon

Ingredients

- ✓ 1 cup cooked rice
- ✓ 1 cup coconut milk
- ✓ 1/2 teaspoon stevia (NuStevia Pure White Powder or SweetLeaf Liquid)
- ✓ 1 tsp ground cardamom
- ✓ 1 tsp ground cinnamon, plus more for garnish

Directions

In a medium saucepan, stir together all ingredients and bring the mixture to a simmer. Cook for 5 minutes stirring frequently until the pudding is thick and creamy.

Serve warm or at room temperature. Garnish, as desired.

Serves 4

Stage Number 1

Lemon Custard

Ingredients

- ✓ 1/2 teaspoon stevia (NuStevia Pure White Powder or SweetLeaf Liquid)
- ✓ 1/2 cup fresh lemon juice
- ✓ 6 Tbs. ghee
- ✓ 1 Tbs. lemon zest
- ✓ 3 large eggs, beaten

Directions

In top of double boiler, over simmering water, cook all ingredients, whisking frequently until a custard forms and bubbles appear on surface, about 10 to 15 minutes.

Remove from heat and strain through a fine mesh sieve into a bowl. Spoon into dessert cups and top with fresh berries.

Chill if desired.

Serves 4

Stage Number 2

Melt In Your Mouth Shortbread

Ingredients

- ✓ 2 cups freshly milled whole grain flour **
- ✓ 1/2 tsp salt
- ✓ 1/2 cup sucanat
- ✓ 1 cup ghee
- ✓ ** Brown Rice Flour is the best to use for this recipe

Directions

Directions

Mix together dry ingredients. Cut in ghee working it in with your hands. Press into a greased 9 X 9 pan. Prick with a fork.

Bake at 350° for 20-25 minutes.

Cut while warm. Store in an airtight container.

Chapter 7

Dips, Dressings & Sauces

Stage Number 1

Creamy Cucumber Dressing

Ingredients

- ✓ 1 large cucumber
- ✓ 2 Tbs. fresh dill or
- ✓ 5 tsp dried dill
- ✓ 1 tsp sea salt
- ✓ 1 Tbs. freshly squeezed lemon juice
- ✓ 1/3 cup expeller pressed safflower oil

Directions

Peel, seed and chop the cucumber into chunks.

Place all ingredients in a blender. Blend thoroughly.

Serve fresh or chilled.

Cooking Tips

It refrigerates well for about a day. You may freeze leftovers

Stage Number 1

Fresh Salsa

Ingredients

- ✓ 2 limes, juiced
- ✓ salt
- ✓ freshly ground black pepper
- ✓ 8-9 fresh tomatoes
- ✓ 2 jalapeño, split and seeded (be careful and wash your hands - it is very hot)
- ✓ 3-4 garlic
- ✓ 1/2 bunch cilantro
- ✓ 1 large onion, chopped in chunks

Directions

Cut the tomatoes in half. Place the tomatoes, onion and jalapeño onto a baking dish. Drizzle with olive oil. Roast in a 450° oven for 30 minutes.

Puree all ingredients until the desired consistency has been met.

Stage Number 1

Garlic Vinaigrette

Ingredients

- ✓ 2 -3 cloves garlic, pressed
- ✓ 1 lemon, juiced
- ✓ salt
- ✓ freshly ground black pepper
- ✓ 1/4 cup extra-virgin olive oil

Directions

Mix the garlic, lemon juice, salt and pepper in a glass bowl. In a slow stream, whisk in the olive oil until combined.

Stage Number 1

Guacamole

Ingredients

- ✓ 5 ripe avocados
- ✓ 6 Tbs. chopped fresh cilantro
- ✓ 1 medium onion, diced
- ✓ 1-3 jalapeno chiles, stemmed, seeded and finely diced (the more you use - the hotter it will be)
- ✓ 1 large tomato, seeded and diced
- ✓ 3 Tbs freshly squeezed lime juice
- ✓ 1 1/2 tsp salt
- ✓ 1/2 tsp freshly ground black pepper

Directions

In a mixing bowl place peeled, quartered and seeded avocados. Mash with a potato masher or fork until chunky.

Add the remaining ingredients and combine with a fork.

Chill and serve.

Stage Number 1

Homemade Mayonnaise

Ingredients

- ✓ 1 large egg yolk
- ✓ 2 TB fresh lemon or lime juice
- ✓ 1 cup, minus 2 Tbs. olive oil or safflower oil
- ✓ 1/2 tsp salt
- ✓ fresh herbs of your choice

Directions

In a food processor or blender, beat egg yolk, juice salt and ¼ cup oil.

With blender or food processor running add remaining oil very slowly in a thin stream, a little at a time. Whisk and blend completely until you reach the desired consistency. Chill in refrigerator.

You may want to shred fresh chives, dill, basil, tarragon or other herbs into mixture before refrigerating.

Cooking TipsCooking Tips

Mayonnaise last 6 to 7 days in refrigerator.

Stage Number 1

Hummus

Ingredients

- ✓ 3 cloves garlic, minced
- ✓ 2 cups cooked garbanzo beans (chick peas)
- ✓ 1/2 cup extra virgin olive oil
- ✓ 1 1/2 tsp sea salt
- ✓ 2 Tbs. freshly squeezed lemon juice

Directions

Place the oil in a blender or food processor. Add one cup of the beans. Puree until mixed, but slightly chunky. Add the second cup of the beans and garlic. Puree until smooth.
Add the salt, lemon juice. Puree until smooth or desired consistency. Serve immediately or refrigerate until ready to serve.

Stage Number 1

Japanese Style Ginger Dressing

Ingredients

- ✓ 1/2 cup minced shallots
- ✓ 1/2 cup oil
- ✓ 1/3 cup lemon juice
- ✓ 3 1/2 Tbs. water
- ✓ 2 Tbs. fresh ginger, minced
- ✓ 2 Tbs. celery, minced
- ✓ 1 Tbs. tomato paste
- ✓ 1 Tbs. Bragg's Amino Acids
- ✓ 2 1/2 tsp honey
- ✓ 1/2 tsp garlic, minced
- ✓ 1/2 tsp salt
- ✓ 1/4 tsp black pepper, ground

Directions

Combine all ingredients in a blender. Blend on high speed for about 30 seconds or until all the ginger is well-pureed.

Taste and adjust seasonings.

Stage Number 1

Lemon Tarragon Aioli

Ingredients

- ✓ 1 clove roasted garlic
- ✓ 1 egg
- ✓ 1 egg yolks
- ✓ 1/2 tsp dry mustard
- ✓ 1 Tbs. lemon juice
- ✓ zest of 1/2 lemon
- ✓ 1 Tbs. fresh tarragon leaves, chopped or
- ✓ 1 tsp dried tarragon
- ✓ 1 1/2 cup olive oil

Directions

In a blender or food processor, place the roasted garlic, egg, egg yolk, mustard, tarragon, lemon zest and lemon juice. Puree until smooth. Add the oil in a slow drizzle until the aioli emulsifies.

Store in an airtight container and refrigerate until ready to use.

Cooking Tips

Will keep for about 4 days.

Stage Number 1

Olive Oil Dipping Sauce

Ingredients

- ✓ 3/4 cup extra virgin olive oil
- ✓ 6 cloves minced garlic
- ✓ 1/2 tsp salt
- ✓ 2 Tbs. Italian seasoning
- ✓ 1/2 tsp red pepper flakes

Directions

Combine ingredients and heat just until garlic begins to sizzle. Remove from heat.

Dip your legal bread as desired or use as a marinade for your favorite meat or poultry.

Stage Number 1

Quick & EZ Tomato Sauce

Ingredients

- ✓ 2 med tomatoes
- ✓ 1 Tbs. ghee
- ✓ 1 clove garlic, minced
- ✓ 1 Tbs. olive oil
- ✓ 1 tsp dried basil
- ✓ 1 tsp dried oregano
- ✓ 1 tsp sea salt

Directions

Heat a skillet on the stove on medium heat. While the skillet is heating, chop the tomatoes. Set the tomatoes aside.

When the skillet is hot, melt the ghee. Add the oil. Heat until hot.

Add the garlic. Cook until it sizzles.

Add the tomatoes. These will fall apart and form a sauce with the butter and oil.

Add the basil, oregano and salt. Cook through. Mash with a fork for a smoother sauce.

Serve over legal pasta.

Serves 6

Cooking Tips

Add a sweet red bell pepper while you are cooking the tomatoes. This gives the sauce a fresh and crunchy consistency and sweetens the flavor.

Stage Number 1

Roasted Vegetable Dip

Ingredients

- ✓ 1 medium eggplant, peeled and cut into chunks
- ✓ 1/4 cup olive oil
- ✓ 2 cups diced onions
- ✓ 2 cloves garlic, chopped
- ✓ 1 Tbs. dried basil
- ✓ 1 Tbs. dried oregano
- ✓ 1 tsp ground cumin
- ✓ 1 Tbs. sweet paprika
- ✓ 2 roasted red bell peppers, roughly chopped or torn
- ✓ 1 Tbs. lemon juice
- ✓ salt
- ✓ freshly ground black pepper

Directions

Before assembling your ingredients, salt the eggplant and let it drain in a colander for 30 minutes, unless you are using young, fresh eggplant. Squeeze out any excess liquid and pat dry.

Heat the olive oil in a medium sauté pan and add the eggplant and onions.

When the vegetables are soft, add the garlic, basil, oregano, cumin and paprika and cook for 5 minutes, or until the aromas are released.

Remove from the heat, and add the roasted peppers.

Transfer the mixture to a food processor and blend until smooth. Finish with the lemon juice and salt and pepper to taste.

Stage Number 2

Spicy Pear Sauce

Ingredients

- ✓ 4 firm pears
- ✓ 1/2 cup raw honey
- ✓ 1/2 cup water
- ✓ 5 whole cloves
- ✓ 1/2 tsp cinnamon

Directions

Peel and chop the pears into small pieces. Set aside.

Bring honey, water, cloves and cinnamon to a boil in a small saucepan. Turn heat to low.

Add the pears and heat until hot. Serve.

Cooking Tips

Refrigerates well for two days.

Stage Number 1

Tomato Italian Herb Dressing

Ingredients

- ✓ 1 large tomatoes
- ✓ 1 clove garlic
- ✓ 1 tsp dried basil
- ✓ 1 tsp dried oregano
- ✓ 1/2 tsp sea salt
- ✓ 1/3 cup expeller pressed safflower oil

Directions

Chop the tomatoes into chunks.

Peel the garlic and place in a small sauce pan. Add the oil. Heat just until the garlic sizzles.

Place the tomatoes, oregano, basil, garlic and salt in a blender.

Puree. With blender going, slowly drizzle in the oil.

Serve immediately or chill. If chilled, mix well before serving.

Cooking Tips

For a super sweet treat, exchange the tomatoes for sun-dried tomatoes packed in olive oil. Oh my goodness!

Chapter 8

Meats

Stage Number 1

Beef Fajitas

Ingredients

- ✓ 4 garlic cloves, minced
- ✓ 1/4 cup fresh lemon juice
- ✓ 1 1/2 tsp ground cumin
- ✓ 2 Tbs. olive oil
- ✓ 1 1/2 lb. skirt steak, trimmed and cut into large pieces to fit on a grill or broiler pan or in a ridged grill pan
- ✓ 1 Tbs. vegetable oil
- ✓ 2 assorted colored bell peppers, sliced thin
- ✓ 1 large red onion, sliced thin
- ✓ 2 garlic cloves, minced

Directions

In a large bowl whisk together the garlic paste, lemon juice, cumin, and olive oil. Add the steak to the marinade, turning it to coat it well, and let it marinate, covered and chilled, for at least 1 hour or overnight.

Grill the steak, drained, on a well-oiled rack set about 5 inches over glowing coals or in a hot well-seasoned ridged grill pan over moderately high heat for 3 to 4 minutes on each side, or until it is just springy to the touch, for medium-rare meat. (Alternatively, the steak may be broiled on the rack of a broiler pan under a preheated broiler about 4 inches from the heat for 3 to 4 minutes on each side for medium-rare meat.)

Transfer the steak to a cutting board and let it stand for 10 minutes.

While the steak is standing, in a large skillet heat the oil over moderately high heat until it is hot but not smoking, add the bell peppers, onion, and garlic, and sauté the mixture, stirring, for 5 minutes, or until the bell peppers are softened.

Slice the steak thinly, across the grain, on the diagonal and arrange the slices on a platter with the bell pepper mixture. Drizzle any steak juices over the steak

Serves 4

Cooking Tips

Since wheat can cause problems for some people with yeast sensitivities, I avoid using flour tortillas. Instead, I prefer to pile the beef, onions and peppers on a bed of shredded lettuce with a large dollop of homemade guacamole on top. Yummy!

Stage Number 1

Beef Lo Mein

Ingredients

- ✓ 12 oz legal noodles
- ✓ 2 tsp sesame oil
- ✓ 2 tsp minced fresh ginger
- ✓ 2 cloves garlic, minced
- ✓ 12 oz grilled beef, cut into 1/4-inch pieces
- ✓ 8 grilled scallions, chopped
- ✓ 1 cup snap peas
- ✓ 1/3 cup shredded carrots
- ✓ 3/4 cup reduced-sodium beef broth
- ✓ 2 -3 Tb Bragg's Amino Acids
- ✓ 1/4 cup chopped fresh cilantro leaves

Directions

Cook noodles according to package directions.

Meanwhile, heat the sesame oil in a large skillet. Add ginger and garlic and sauté 1 minute.

Add beef, scallions, snap peas and carrots and sauté 1 minute.

Add broth and amino acids and bring to a simmer and cook 5 minutes, until carrots are soft.

Drain noodles and add to sauce. Toss together with cilantro.

Serves 4

Stage Number 1

Braised Beef, Peppers & Onions: Ropa Vieja Style

Ingredients

- ✓ 5 Tbs. olive oil
- ✓ 3 lb. skirt or flank steak, cut into large pieces
- ✓ 2 bay leaves
- ✓ 1/2 onion, peeled and studded with 4 whole cloves
- ✓ Kosher salt and freshly ground black pepper
- ✓ 2 green bell peppers, seeded and thinly sliced
- ✓ 2 red bell peppers, seeded and thinly sliced
- ✓ 3 garlic cloves, roughly chopped
- ✓ 1 red onion, thinly sliced
- ✓ 1 tsp dried oregano
- ✓ 1 tsp ground cumin
- ✓ 3 Tbs. tomato paste
- ✓ 1 (14 to 16-ounce) can whole tomatoes with juice, chopped
- ✓ 1 cup frozen peas, thawed

Directions

Heat 2 tablespoons of olive oil in a large skillet over medium-high heat. Season the steak with salt and pepper and cook, turning once, until well browned.

Transfer the steak with 1 bay leaf and the clove-studded onion to a large pot, with a tight-fitting lid, and cover with water by 1 inch. Bring to a boil, lower the heat, and simmer, covered, until tender, about 1 1/2 hours. Remove from the heat and cool the meat in the liquid for about 30 minutes. Transfer meat to a platter and cover, to keep warm. Reserve 2 cups of the cooking liquid. (Stew may be made up to this point 1 day ahead.)

Meanwhile, return the skillet to medium-high heat and heat the remaining 3 tablespoons oil. Add the remaining bay leaf, peppers, garlic, onion, oregano, and cumin and cook, stirring, until softened and fragrant, about 8 minutes. Add the tomato paste and cook, stirring, until dark red, about 1 minute more. Add the 2 cups reserved liquid, tomatoes, and olives and bring to a boil. Lower the heat and simmer until slightly thickened, about 10 minutes.

While the vegetables are cooking, pull the steak into shreds. Add the steak and peas to the vegetable mixture and cook, stirring, until just heated through. Season with salt and pepper, to taste. Serve with rice.

Serves 8

Stage Number 1

Dry Rubbed Flank Steak

Ingredients

- ✓ 1 Tbs. ground mustard
- ✓ 1 Tbs. onion powder
- ✓ 1 Tbs. garlic powder
- ✓ 1 Tbs. salt
- ✓ 1/2 tsp cayenne
- ✓ 1/4 tsp allspice
- ✓ 3 lb. flank steak

Directions

Preheat a grill pan over high heat for 3 to 4 minutes

Combine the mustard, onion powder, garlic powder, salt, cayenne and allspice in a small bowl. Rub the flank steak all over with the mix and let sit for 10 minutes.

Put the steak on the hot grill and cook 5 minutes per side. Remove and let rest 10 minutes before slicing.

Stage Number 1

Garlic & Ghee Pinwheel Steaks

Ingredients

Filling:
- ✓ 1 shallot, chopped
- ✓ 1/2 cup parsley, chopped
- ✓ 2 cloves garlic, minced
- ✓ Salt and pepper
- ✓ 1/2 cup ghee

Steaks:
- ✓ 3 thin cut (3/4-inch) New York strip steaks
- ✓ Coarse salt and black pepper
- ✓ Extra-virgin olive oil, for drizzling
- ✓ Metal skewers

Directions

Preheat oven to 500° degrees F.

Place 2 pinches salt, a few grinds black pepper, ghee and garlic in a food processor. Pulse grind the filling into a paste. Taste and adjust seasonings. Remove 1/2 cup of filling paste to a bowl and stir in extra-virgin olive oil to loosen it. Reserve remaining filling in processor bowl.

Place steaks between layers of waxed paper several inches apart. Pound steaks with a heavy bottomed pan to 1/2 their thickness. Season each steak with salt and pepper on both sides. Cover each steak with a thin layer of filling. Roll steaks tightly and cut each steak in half crosswise. Secure pinwheels with a carefully placed skewer and set 6 pinwheels on a baking sheet. Drizzle with extra-virgin oil and roast 12 to 15 minutes. Remove skewers and transfer pinwheels to dinner plates. Top each with a generous portion of reserved sauce made from filling and extra-virgin olive oil, combined.

Serves 6

Stage Number 1

Homemade Breakfast Sausage

Making your own sausage allows you to choose the freshest ingredients available and to avoid the use of nitrates and refined ingredients.

Ingredients

- ✓ 1 pound pork or beef, ground
- ✓ 1/4 to 1 tsp sage
- ✓ 1/4 tsp marjoram
- ✓ 1/4 tsp thyme
- ✓ 1/4 tsp coriander seed, ground
- ✓ 1 tsp salt
- ✓ 1/8 tsp freshly ground black pepper
- ✓ 1 to 3 Tbs. Water

Directions

To Make The Sausage Blend:

Sprinkle the seasonings over the ground meat. Knead until thoroughly blended. Make into patties, a meatloaf or stuff into sausage casings by hand or with a sausage horn.

Refrigerate in airtight containers for 2 or 3 days to allow flavors to blend.

To Cook The Sausage:

Loaf: Set loaf pan in another pan of hot water in oven. Bake at 350° for 1 1/2 hours or until meat thermometer reaches 160°.

Patties: Fry until golden brown.

Rolls or links: Cover with water in fry pan. Simmer for 20 to 30 minutes. Drain water and dry until golden brown.

Cooking Tips

Your sausage will only be good for 2-3 days in the refrigerator. If not using immediately, freeze for up to 2 months.

Stage Number 1

Homemade Italian Sausage

Making your own sausage allows you to choose the freshest ingredients available and to avoid the use of nitrates and refined ingredients.

Ingredients

- ✓ 1 pound pork or 1/2 pork and 1/2 beef, ground
- ✓ 1 medium onion, minced
- ✓ 1 1/2 tsp salt
- ✓ 1 clove garlic, minced
- ✓ 1 bay leaf, finely crumbled
- ✓ 1/2 tsp pepper
- ✓ 1/2 tsp fennel seed, crushed
- ✓ 1/4 tsp paprika
- ✓ 1/8 tsp thyme
- ✓ 1/8 tsp cayenne pepper

Directions

To Make The Sausage Blend:

Sprinkle the seasonings over the ground meat. Knead until thoroughly blended. Make into patties, a meatloaf or stuff into sausage casings by hand or with a sausage horn.

Refrigerate in airtight containers for 2 or 3 days to allow flavors to blend.

To Cook The Sausage:

Loaf: Set loaf pan in another pan of hot water in oven. Bake at 350° for 1 1/2 hours or until meat thermometer reaches 160°.

Patties: Fry until golden brown.

Rolls or links: Cover with water in fry pan. Simmer for 20 to 30 minutes. Drain water and dry until golden brown.

Cooking Tips

Your sausage will only be good for 2-3 days in the refrigerator. If not using immediately, freeze for up to 2 months.

Stage Number 1

Homemade Polish Kielbasa

Ingredients

- ✓ 2 pounds coarsely ground pork butt
- ✓ 3/4 pound finely ground beef
- ✓ 1 1/2 tsp coarse salt
- ✓ 1 1/2 tsp crushed peppercorns
- ✓ 1 1/2 tsp marjoram
- ✓ 1 Tbs. paprika
- ✓ 2 cloves garlic, minced
- ✓ 1 tsp honey
- ✓ 1/2 tsp ground nutmeg

Directions

To Make The Sausage Blend:

Sprinkle the seasonings over the ground meat. Knead until thoroughly blended. Make into patties, a meatloaf or stuff into sausage casings by hand or with a sausage horn.

Refrigerate in airtight containers for 2 or 3 days to allow flavors to blend.

To Cook The Sausage:

Loaf: Set loaf pan in another pan of hot water in oven. Bake at 350° for 1 1/2 hours or until meat thermometer reaches 160°.

Patties: Fry until golden brown.

Rolls or links: Cover with water in fry pan. Simmer for 20 to 30 minutes. Drain water and dry until golden brown.

Cooking Tips

Your sausage will only be good for 2-3 days in the refrigerator. If not using immediately, freeze for up to 2 months.

Stage Number 1

Jamaican Jerk Flank Steak

Ingredients

- ✓ extra virgin olive oil
- ✓ 1/2 cup lemon juice
- ✓ 1 Tbs. honey
- ✓ 2 tsp ground allspice
- ✓ 2 tsp ground cloves
- ✓ 2 tsp dried basil
- ✓ 1/2 tsp red pepper flakes
- ✓ 2 tsp dried thyme
- ✓ 2 1/2 lb. flank steak
- ✓ Salt and pepper

Directions

Preheat grill, grill pan or broiler. Coat a grill pan, large baking sheet or shallow roasting pan with oil.

In a shallow dish, whisk together juice, honey, allspice, cloves, basil, thyme, pepper flakes, salt, and pepper. Add flank steak and turn to coat (you may marinate up to 24 hours at this point).

Transfer flank steak to prepared pan and pour over any remaining marinade. Grill or broil 5 minutes per side, until medium-rare. Let stand 10 minutes before slicing crosswise into thin slices.

Serves 4

Stage Number 1

Oriental London Broil

Ingredients

- ✓ 6 Tbs. Cold Pressed Extra Virgin Olive Oil
- ✓ 3 Tbs. Bragg's Amino Acids
- ✓ 1 tsp Ground Ginger
- ✓ 1/2 tsp Cumin
- ✓ 1 tsp Onion Powder
- ✓ 1/4 tsp Real Salt or Sea Salt
- ✓ 1/4 tsp Sweet Paprika
- ✓ 30 drops Clear Stevia Liquid
- ✓ Juice of 1 Lemon

Directions

Mix all ingredients.

Trim the meat of all the fat and score the top in crisscrossed diagonals. Marinate the London Broil for 30 minutes to several hours.

Grill on a Med/Hot Grill or Broil about 8-10 minutes each side or until center temperature meets 140° - 160°.

Let stand for a few minutes for the juices to redistribute throughout the meat. Slice very thin on the diagonal.

Stage Number 1

Peppercorn Steak

Ingredients

- ✓ 2 Tbs. olive oil
- ✓ 2 tsp cracked peppercorn
- ✓ 1 clove minced garlic
- ✓ 1 tsp dried rosemary
- ✓ 4 ribeye steaks
- ✓ 1/4 tsp salt

Directions

Combine oil, peppercorns, garlic and herbs in a small bowl. Rub mixture on both sides of each steak. Cover and refrigerate.

Prepare grill for direct cooking.

Place steaks on grid over medium heat. Grill, uncovered, 10 to 12 minutes for medium-rare to medium doneness, turning occasionally. Season with salt after cooking.

Serves 4

Stage Number 1

Swiss Steak

Ingredients

- ✓ Cooking spray, as needed
- ✓ 1 lb. round steak, cut into 4 equal portions with fat removed
- ✓ 1 8 oz. can tomato sauce
- ✓ 1/3 cup water
- ✓ 1 Tbs. Bragg's Amino Acids
- ✓ 1/4 cup diced onion
- ✓ 1/2 tsp salt
- ✓ 1/8 tsp freshly ground black pepper
- ✓ 1/2 tsp crushed oregano
- ✓ 1 Tbs. dried parsley flakes
- ✓ 1 8 ½ oz can peas, drained, rinsed

Directions

Warm a large nonstick skillet coated with cooking spray over medium-high heat. Add steak and brown on both sides. Drain off any fat.

In a small bowl, combine tomato sauce, water, Worcestershire sauce, onion, salt, pepper, oregano, and parsley; mix well. Pour over meat in skillet, cover, and simmer for 30 minutes or until meat is tender.

Gently stir in peas and cook an additional 2 to 3 minutes until peas are thoroughly heated.

Serves 4

Stage Number 1

Tamale Pie

Ingredients

Tamale Pie Filling:
- ✓ 2 cups crushed tomatoes, canned
- ✓ 1 pound ground beef
- ✓ 1/4 tsp garlic powder
- ✓ 2 Tbs. onion powder
- ✓ 1/2 tsp celery seed
- ✓ 2 cups corn
- ✓ 1 tsp salt
- ✓ 2 Tbs. chili powder

Cornmeal Crust:
- ✓ 1 cup cornmeal
- ✓ 1/2 tsp salt
- ✓ 1/2 tsp chili powder
- ✓ 1 cup water
- ✓ 1 3/4 cups beef broth

Directions

Preheat oven to 375°.

Brown meat on medium heat. Drain fat.

Add remaining filling ingredients. Simmer uncovered on low heat for 10 minutes.

Measure into 1 1/2 quart sauce pan cornmeal, salt and chili powder. Stir in the broth and water. Cook over low heat, stirring constantly till mixture becomes very thick.

Press 1/2 of the cornmeal crust into a greased casserole dish.

Add tamale filling.

Top with remaining cornmeal mixture.

Bake at 375° for 40 minutes.

Chapter 9

Poultry

Stage Number 1

Chicken with 20 Cloves of Garlic

Around our house this dish is better known as Halloween Chicken, because it keeps the vampires away. And, possibly anyone else who did not eat it with you. Lots of garlic, but oh, so good!

Ingredients

- ✓ 6 fresh boneless, skinless chicken breasts
- ✓ 1 tsp coarse salt
- ✓ 1 tsp freshly ground pepper
- ✓ 1/4 cup olive oil
- ✓ 20 cloves garlic, peeled
- ✓ 1/2 cup chopped fresh parsley

Directions

Preheat oven to 400°F.

Season chicken all over with salt and pepper. Drizzle with oil and arrange in a single layer in a 13x9-inch baking dish. Scatter garlic cloves over chicken. Cover and bake 20 minutes.

Sprinkle with parsley and bake, uncovered, 10 minutes longer.

Let rest for 5 minutes and serve with brown rice drenched in the pan juices. Make sure to include a few of the roasted garlic cloves on each person's plate.

Serves 6

Stage Number 1

Chicken Drummers

Ingredients

- ✓ 2 pounds chicken drummets
- ✓ 1/3 cup olive oil
- ✓ 3 lemons, juiced
- ✓ 10 cloves garlic, pressed
- ✓ 10 sprigs fresh thyme leaves
- ✓ 1 bunch flat-leaf parsley, chopped
- ✓ 1 Tbs. dried rosemary
- ✓ 1/2 tsp cayenne pepper
- ✓ 1 tsp paprika
- ✓ salt
- ✓ freshly ground black pepper

Directions

Combine all the ingredients in a noncorrosive bowl. Let marinate for 1 hour or more.

Heat a grill until very hot. Place the drummets on the grill and cook for about 10 minutes, turning constantly. They should become nicely charred from the olive oil in the marinade.

Stage Number 1

Chicken Fajitas

Ingredients

- ✓ 1/4 cup fresh lime juice
- ✓ 4 cloves garlic, peeled and smashed
- ✓ 2 Tbs. roughly chopped cilantro leaves
- ✓ 2 Tbs. extra virgin olive oil
- ✓ 2 tsp Bragg's Amino Acids
- ✓ 1 tsp dried crushed Mexican oregano
- ✓ 1 tsp red pepper flakes
- ✓ 1 tsp ground cumin
- ✓ 1 Tbs. minced garlic
- ✓ 1 tsp ground coriander
- ✓ 2 lb. chicken, cut bite size slices
- ✓ 2 tsp salt
- ✓ 1 tsp ground black pepper
- ✓ 1 red bell pepper, stemmed, seeded, and thinly sliced
- ✓ 1 green bell pepper, stemmed, seeded, and thinly sliced
- ✓ 1 large onion, cut into thin slices
- ✓ 1 yellow bell pepper, stemmed, seeded, and thinly sliced
- ✓ 1 large white onion, thinly sliced
- ✓ Lime wedges, accompaniment

Directions

In a bowl, whisk together the lime juice, garlic, cilantro, 1 tablespoon of the oil, the Bragg's amino acids, oregano, pepper flakes, cumin and coriander. Pour into a large zip-lock bag, add the chicken, and seal. Place in a baking dish and refrigerate for at least 1 hour, turning occasionally. Add the onions and peppers to the marinade and refrigerate for another hour.

Remove the chicken, onions and peppers from the bag and season with 1 teaspoon of the salt and 1/2 teaspoon of the pepper.

Preheat the grill to high.

Cook the chicken mixture over the grill in a cast iron skillet for about 12-20 minutes or until cooked through. Remove from the heat and let rest for 5 minutes before serving.

Squeeze with lime juice and serve immediately.

Serves 6

Stage Number 1

Chicken with Sage

Ingredients

- ✓ 4 boneless, skinless chicken breasts
- ✓ salt
- ✓ freshly ground black pepper
- ✓ 3 lemons, juiced
- ✓ 6 Tbs olive oil
- ✓ 40 fresh sage leaves or
- ✓ 2 tsp dried sage
- ✓ 4 Tbs ghee

Directions

n a hot skillet, add olive oil and ghee. Add the sage for 30 seconds, then add the chicken breast. Cook for 7 minutes on each side, or until cooked through.

Serve with the oil/butter/sage mixture poured over the top of the chicken once plated.

Serves 4

Stage Number 1

Deep-Fried Cajun Turkey

Ingredients

- ✓ 1 Large canister of Cajun Seasoning
- ✓ 1 12 lb. Turkey or Turkey Breast
- ✓ 4-5 gal. Peanut Oil (Safflower Oil will work if nuts are not allowed by your doctor)

Directions

Remove turkey from the wrappings and clean very good inside and outside. Put in a large pan and pat Cajun seasoning all over the outside of the bird. Let it sit in the refrigerator for several hours (the longer the better).

Put a very large stock pot on the grill or if you have a side burner on your grill use that. Fill it ½ - ¾ full with oil. Be careful to not over fill it, or when you put the turkey into the pot the oil will flow over the sides and ignite in the flames. When the oil is very hot, carefully slide the turkey into the pot. Fry the turkey for 45 minutes to 1 hour or until a meat thermometer inserted into the breast register 170°F. Another way to check for doneness is to watch for the turkey to "float." Remove from oil and let drain and cool slightly before slicing.

Make sure that you get a bite of the well seasoned and crispy outside. So Good!

Cooking Tips

Make sure that the turkey is fully thawed before you add it to the oil. A frozen turkey can cause an explosion in the oil and a fire. Also be careful to not over fill the stockpot with oil. It will overflow and can ignite when the turkey is added. User extreme caution.

Stage Number 1

French Inspired Chicken

Ingredients

- ✓ 2 1/2 lb. boneless, skinless chicken breasts, cut into large chunks
- ✓ 6 shallots, chopped
- ✓ 2 Tbs. tarragon, chopped
- ✓ 3 Tbs. ghee
- ✓ 1/2 cup chicken broth

Directions

Preheat oven to 450° F.

Arrange chicken in a baking dish, 9 by 13-inch.

Add shallots, ghee, tarragon and salt and pepper to the dish. Toss and coat the chicken with all ingredients, then place in oven. Roast 20 minutes.

Add broth to the dish and combine with pan juices. Return to oven and turn oven off. Let stand 5 minutes longer then remove chicken from the oven. Place baking dish on trivet and serve, spooning pan juices over the chicken pieces.

Serves 4

Stage Number 1

Honey Lime Chicken

Ingredients

- ✓ 1/4 cup extra virgin olive oil
- ✓ 1 Tbs. honey
- ✓ 1 Tbs. lime juice
- ✓ 1/4 tsp paprika
- ✓ 4 chicken breast halves, washed and patted dry

Directions

Preheat oven to 400° degrees.

In a small bowl, combine the oil, honey, lime juice, and paprika.

Place chicken, skin side up, in a baking dish. Apply mixture to chicken pieces in a single layer.

Bake in oven for 35-40 minutes, basting every 8-10 minutes, until well browned and juices run clear when you prick the skin.

Remove from oven. Cover and let rest for 15 minutes before serving.

This softens the chicken and keeps it hot until served.

Serves 4

Stage Number 1

Stir-Fried Chicken & Vegetables

Ingredients

- ✓ 1 Tbs. safflower oil
- ✓ 2 to 3 cloves garlic, minced
- ✓ 1 Tbs. minced fresh ginger
- ✓ 1 lb. boneless, skinless chicken breasts, cut into strips
- ✓ 1 medium onion, diced
- ✓ 2 cups sliced carrots
- ✓ 1 red bell pepper, seeded and sliced into thin strips
- ✓ 2 cups sugar snap peas
- ✓ 1 15-ounce can baby corn, drained
- ✓ 2 cups broccoli florets
- ✓ 1/4 cup Bragg's Amino Acids
- ✓ 2 tsp cornstarch
- ✓ 1 cup reduced-sodium chicken broth

Directions

Heat oil in a wok or large skillet over medium-high heat.

Add garlic and ginger and cook 1 minute.

Add chicken and cook 3 to 4 minutes, until starting to brown, stirring constantly.

Add onions, carrots, and peppers and cook 1 minute.

Add snap peas, corn and broccoli and cook 2 minutes.

Add Bragg's and cook 2 minutes, until vegetables are crisp-tender.

Dissolve cornstarch or arrowroot in chicken broth in a small bowl and add to wok. Simmer 2 minutes, until sauce thickens. Serve with fried rice.

Serves 4

Chapter 10

Salads

Stage Number 1

Baby Black Lentil Salad

Ingredients

- ✓ 4 cups cooked baby black lentils, cooled
- ✓ 2 shallots, finely diced
- ✓ 1 cucumber, peeled, seeded and diced
- ✓ 1 tomato, seeded and diced
- ✓ 2 scallions, diced
- ✓ 1 Tbs. mint leaves, julienned
- ✓ 1/2 lime, juiced
- ✓ 2 Tbs. extra virgin olive oil
- ✓ salt
- ✓ freshly ground black pepper

Directions

Combine all the ingredients in a mixing bowl. Gently toss until the lentils are well coated.

Garnish with extra mint and serve.

Serves 8

Stage Number 1

Bite Sized Veggie Salad

Ingredients

- ✓ 7 seedless cucumbers
- ✓ 4-5 tomatoes, seeded
- ✓ 1 green bell peppers, seeded
- ✓ 3 scallions
- ✓ 4 radishes
- ✓ salt
- ✓ freshly ground black pepper
- ✓ olive oil

Directions

Finely dice all the vegetables into a uniform size.

Toss with olive oil, salt and pepper.

Serve immediately or refrigerate until ready to serve.

Serves 6

Stage Number 1

Evelyn's Potato Shrimp Salad

My grandmother made this salad for us often during the summer. It still brings back memories of her.

Ingredients

- ✓ 1 pound shrimp, cooked and chopped
- ✓ 1 pound potatoes, diced and cooked
- ✓ 1 bell peppers, chopped
- ✓ 2 green onions, chopped
- ✓ 2 celery, chopped
- ✓ 1 cup homemade mayonnaise
- ✓ squeeze of lemon juice, to taste

Directions

Cook the shrimp in boiling water with some seafood seasoning until pink. Drain. Cool and chop into bite size pieces.

Peel and dice the potatoes. Cook them in salted boiling water just until they are fork tender. Drain and cool.

Mix all ingredients together. Chill.

Serves 4

Stage Number 1

Mixed Greens with a Lime Vinaigrette

Ingredients

- ✓ 6 cups mixed lettuce greens
- ✓ 4 Tbs. extra virgin olive oil
- ✓ 2 Tbs. fresh lime juice
- ✓ 1/2 tsp dry mustard
- ✓ 1-2 cloves garlic, minced
- ✓ 1/4 tsp ground cumin
- ✓ 1/4 tsp salt
- ✓ 1/4 tsp ground black pepper

Directions

Place lettuce in a large bowl.

In a small bowl, combine all of the dressing ingredients except the oil. Slowly whisk the oil into the dressing.

Pour desired amount of vinaigrette over greens just before serving.

Serves 4

Stage Number 1

Nancy's French-Style Green Bean Salad

This was my mother's special summer salad. I don't know how much of this satisfying salad I have gobbled up over the years.

Ingredients

- ✓ 2 cans French-style green beans, drained
- ✓ 2 tsp lemon juice
- ✓ 1/8 tsp salt
- ✓ 2 1/3 Tbs. homemade mayonnaise
- ✓ 1 1/3 Tbs. onion, chopped

Directions

Mix all ingredients except green beans to form a dressing.

Pour over the beans and toss well. Chill and serve.

Serves 4

Stage Number 1

Pimento Corn Salad

Ingredients

- ✓ 2 cups fresh, frozen or canned corn, thawed and/or drained
- ✓ 4 oz canned pimento, diced or
- ✓ 1 small red pepper, sautéed in olive oil
- ✓ 1 (4-ounce) can diced green chiles, optional
- ✓ 1 tsp ground cumin
- ✓ Salt and ground black pepper
- ✓ 1 Tbs. chopped parsley leaves

Directions

In a medium bowl, combine corn, pimento, green chiles, and cumin.

Mix well and season to taste with salt and black pepper.

Garnish with fresh parsley.

Serves 4

Stage Number 1

Simple Avocado Salad

Ingredients

- ✓   2 ripe avocados
- ✓   1 lime, juiced
- ✓   1/3 cup fresh cilantro leaves

Directions

Cut avocados in half and remove pit.

Peel flesh away and slice avocado into wedges. Arrange slices on a serving plate.

Squeeze lime juice over avocado slices and then top with torn cilantro leaves.

Serves 2

Stage Number 1

Taco Salad

This is one of my families favorites. I usually at least double the recipe and freeze the extra.

Ingredients

- ✓ 2 Tbs. oil
- ✓ 1 medium onion, chopped
- ✓ 5 cloves garlic, pressed
- ✓ 1 pound ground beef
- ✓ 1 tsp paprika
- ✓ 1 tsp ground cumin seed
- ✓ 1/2 tsp dried oregano
- ✓ 1/2 tsp chili powder
- ✓ 1/2 tsp cayenne pepper, crushed
- ✓ salt
- ✓ freshly ground black pepper
- ✓ 1 cup water
- ✓ 6 oz tomato paste
- ✓ 1 head romaine lettuce
- ✓ 2 medium tomatoes, chopped

Directions

In a large skillet over medium heat, heat the oil. Add the onion and cook until translucent, about 4 minutes. Add the garlic and cook for 1 minute longer. Turn up the heat to high and add the ground beef.

Brown the meat, stirring constantly, until crumbly, about 4 minutes. Drain excess fat. Lower heat and add the paprika, cumin, oregano, chili powder, cayenne, and plenty of salt and pepper.

Add the water and tomato paste, blending well. Bring to a boil, then reduce the heat to low and simmer for 10 minutes, stirring occasionally.

To assemble the salad, place the lettuce on 4 plates. Spoon the mixture over the lettuce. Top with tomatoes, green chilies, green onions and whatever else you like that you are allowed.

Serves 4

Chapter 11

Seafood

Stage Number 1

Awesome Shrimp on the Barbie

Ingredients

- ✓ 1/2 cup ghee, melted
- ✓ 1/2 cup extra virgin olive oil
- ✓ 1/2 cup minced fresh herbs (parsley, thyme, cilantro)
- ✓ 3 Tbs. fresh lemon juice
- ✓ 4 cloves garlic, crushed
- ✓ 1 Tbs. minced shallots
- ✓ salt
- ✓ fresh ground pepper
- ✓ 1 1/2 lb. medium to large shrimp (peeled with tails left on)

Directions

Combine all ingredients except the shrimp.

Add the shrimp and mix.

Marinate at room temperature for at least one hour, stirring occasionally.

Prepare barbecue with medium-hot coals.

Skewer the shrimp.

Grill until opaque (about 2 minutes per side).

Serves 2

Stage Number 1

Perfect Salmon & Potatoes

Ingredients

- ✓ 3 Tbs. Olive Oil
- ✓ 2 Tbs. Bragg's Amino Acids
- ✓ 2 Tbs. Fresh Squeezed Lemon Juice
- ✓ 1 tsp Dried Rosemary
- ✓ 3 tsp Chopped Fresh Ginger or
- ✓ 1 tsp Dried Ground Ginger
- ✓ 1/4 tsp Garlic Powder
- ✓ 1/4 tsp Ground Cumin
- ✓ 1/4 tsp Ground Black Pepper
- ✓ 4 Fresh Salmon Fillets without skin
- ✓ 5-6 Medium to Large sized Red Potatoes
- ✓ Olive Oil
- ✓ Lemon Oil
- ✓ Salt
- ✓ Pepper
- ✓ Thyme
- ✓ Garlic Powder

Directions

Combine the first 9 ingredients. Stir well. Add Salmon and marinate for 30 minutes to a couple of hours.

Using a mandolin or a very sharp knife, slice the potatoes thinly into circles. Lay the slices on an oiled baking sheet in two slightly overlapping lines about 5-6 inches long and about 4 inches wide. Repeat with the remaining potatoes to make enough piles for each salmon fillet.

Season the potatoes with plenty of salt & pepper. Pour a nice drizzle of olive oil mixed with a bit of lemon oil or fresh lemon juice over the beds. Then sprinkle with a touch of thyme and garlic powder.

Bake the potatoes at 425°F for about 30 minutes. Don't let them get too brown. Remove from oven. Leave the potatoes in place on the baking sheet. Reduce oven temperature to 400°F. Carefully lift the Salmon out of the marinade with a large spatula. Lay a fillet on top of each bed of potatoes. Bake for 16-18 minutes, depending on the thickness of the fillets. Remove from oven and squeeze with a bit of lemon juice.

To serve, carefully lift a potato bed with fillet on top and place on plate intact. Serve with a dollop of garlic mayonnaise, which is just homemade mayo with a healthy bit of garlic added, to taste.

Serves 4

Stage Number 1

Spicy Seared Scallops

Ingredients

- ✓ 1 1/2 lb. large scallops, cleaned
- ✓ 2 tsp paprika
- ✓ 1 tsp dried oregano
- ✓ 2 tsp Cajun seasoning
- ✓ 1/4 tsp salt
- ✓ 1/4 tsp pepper
- ✓ 1 Tbs. olive oil
- ✓ nonstick spray

Directions

Combine all the ingredients in a re-sealable plastic bag and marinate in the refrigerator for no more than 1 hour.

Heat a cast-iron griddle until very hot. Lightly spray griddle with nonstick spray or coat with olive oil.

Remove scallops from plastic bag and arrange on the hot griddle so that the scallops are not too close together.

Cook for about 2 minutes on each side depending on thickness and then remove from heat.

Serves 4

Stage Number 1

Steamed Alaskan King Crab Claws

Ingredients

- ✓ 6 Alaskan king crab claws, thawed
- ✓ 2 sprigs dill

Directions

If necessary to fit in microwave, cut claws at joints. Wrap 3 claws at a time in a damp paper towel, along with 1 sprig of dill, and then wrap in plastic wrap. Place wrapped claws in microwave 1 package at a time and cook on high for 2 minutes. Remove and unwrap carefully. Serve immediately.

Serves 2

Stage Number 1

Super Fast Fire Fish

Ingredients

- ✓ 2 Fish fillets (orange roughy; snapper; etc)
- ✓ 1 can Mexican-Style tomatoes, (you choose the heat)

Directions

Put both fillets into skillet.

Cover with Mexican-Style tomatoes, juice and all.

Let sit for 5 minutes so juice permeates fish.

Cover skillet. Cook fish on medium-low for 10 minutes.

Serve without juices.

Serves 2

Stage Number 1

The Family's Favorite Fish & Potatoes

Getting my family to eat fish is usually not possible. But, one day when all I could find in the refrigerator were hash browns and fish fillets, I came up with this throw together meal. To my utter amazement, they ate every bite and asked me to make it again soon. Now, each time I make this dish, they gobble it down. And, it's so easy.

Ingredients

- ✓ 1 pkg. frozen organic hash browns, thawed and dried
- ✓ 1 small onion, minced or
- ✓ 1 tsp onion powder
- ✓ 1/3 cup ghee
- ✓ 4 fish fillets, preferably wild tilapia
- ✓ 1 lemon
- ✓ salt
- ✓ pepper
- ✓ onion powder

Directions

Preheat oven to 450° F.

Place ghee in a glass 9 X 13 baking dish and place in oven until the ghee is melted.

Add the thawed and dried hash browns to the dish. Sprinkle the onions or onion powder over the top. Season with salt and pepper. Bake for 20 minutes or until beginning to turn golden brown around edges.

Season the fish fillets with salt, pepper and onion powder on one side. Place the fish fillets on top of the hash browns, season side down. Season the other side of the fish. Squeeze the lemon over the top of the fish and potatoes.

Return to oven and bake for 4 to 5 minutes. Turn the fish over and bake until light brown and cooked through, about 5 more minutes depending on thickness of fillet.

Serve by using a large spatula to scoop up hash browns with a fillet on top and place on serving platter.

Serves 4

Chapter 12

Seasonings

Stage Number 1

Cajun Seasoning

Ingredients

- ✓ 2 1/2 Tbs. paprika
- ✓ 2 Tbs. salt
- ✓ 2 Tbs. garlic powder
- ✓ 1 Tbs. black pepper
- ✓ 1 Tbs. onion powder
- ✓ 1 Tbs. cayenne pepper
- ✓ 1 Tbs. dried leaf oregano
- ✓ 1 Tbs. dried thyme

Directions

Combine all ingredients thoroughly and store in an airtight jar or container.

Stage Number 1

Chili Powder

Ingredients

- ✓ 3 Tbs. paprika
- ✓ 1 Tbs. ground cumin
- ✓ 2 Tbs. oregano
- ✓ 1 tsp red or cayenne pepper
- ✓ 1/2 tsp garlic powder

Directions

Mix well. Place in an airtight container. Adjust red pepper to taste for a hot or mild blend.

Stage Number 1

Curry Powder

Ingredients

- ✓ 2 Tbs. coriander seeds
- ✓ 1 Tbs. cumin seeds
- ✓ 1 tsp fennel seeds
- ✓ 1/2 tsp whole cloves
- ✓ 1/2 tsp mustard seeds
- ✓ 1 Tbs. cardamom seeds
- ✓ 1 Tbs. whole black peppercorns
- ✓ 2 dried red chiles, broken in pieces, seeds discarded
- ✓ 1 Tbs. turmeric

Directions

Toast the whole spices (coriander, cumin, fennel, cloves, mustard, cardamom and peppercorns) and the chiles in a small dry skillet over medium-low heat, shaking the pan often to prevent them from burning. Toast for a couple of minutes until the spices smell fragrant.

In a clean coffee grinder, grind the toasted spices together to a fine powder. Add the turmeric and give it another quick buzz to combine. Use the spice blend immediately, or store in a sealed jar for as long as 1 month.

Stage Number 1

Ghee

Ingredients

✓ 1 lb. unsalted butter

Directions

Put the butter in a heavy saucepan over moderate heat, swirl the pot around to ensure that it melts slowly and does not sizzle or brown. Increase the heat and bring the butter to a boil.

When the surface is covered with foam, stir gently and reduce the heat to the lowest possible setting. Gently simmer, uncovered, and undisturbed for 45 minutes, until the milk solids in the bottom of the pan have turned golden brown and the butter on top is transparent.

Strain the ghee through a sieve lined with several layers of cheesecloth. The ghee should be perfectly clear and smell nutty; pour into a glass jar and seal tightly.

Stage Number 1

Seafood Seasoning

Ingredients

- ✓ 1 Tbs. ground bay leaves
- ✓ 2 1/2 tsp celery salt
- ✓ 1 1/2 tsp ground mustard seed
- ✓ 1 1/2 tsp black pepper
- ✓ 3/4 tsp ground nutmeg
- ✓ 1/2 tsp ground cloves
- ✓ 1/2 tsp ground ginger
- ✓ 1/2 tsp paprika
- ✓ 1/2 tsp red pepper
- ✓ 1/4 tsp ground mace
- ✓ 1/4 tsp ground cardamom

Directions

Combine and store in an airtight container.

Cooking Tips

Use on seafood, poultry, salads, meats, and more. Makes delicious boiled crabs and shrimp. Try it on French fries, too.

Stage Number 1

Southwest Seasoning

Ingredients

- ✓ 2 Tbs. chili powder
- ✓ 2 tsp ground cumin
- ✓ 2 Tbs. paprika
- ✓ 1 tsp black pepper
- ✓ 1 Tbs. ground coriander
- ✓ 1 tsp cayenne pepper
- ✓ 1 Tbs. garlic powder
- ✓ 1 tsp crushed red pepper
- ✓ 1 Tbs. salt
- ✓ 1 Tbs. dried oregano

Directions

Combine all ingredients thoroughly.

Stage Number 1

Spice Mix for Grilled Vegetables

Ingredients

- ✓ 2 Tbs. Hungarian sweet paprika
- ✓ 1 tsp freshly ground black pepper
- ✓ 1 tsp dried thyme leaves
- ✓ 1 tsp dried rosemary
- ✓ 2 tsp garlic powder
- ✓ 1/2 tsp ground chipotle pepper

Directions

In a spice mill or using a mortar and pestle combine spices and grind until thyme and rosemary are pulverized. Sprinkle a little on prepared vegetables about 1 hour before grilling to marinate them. Grill as usual.

Stage Number 1

Taco Seasoning

Ingredients

- ✓ 2 tsp onion powder
- ✓ 1 tsp salt
- ✓ 1 tsp chili powder
- ✓ ½ tsp cornstarch
- ✓ ¼ tsp cayenne pepper
- ✓ ½ tsp garlic powder
- ✓ ¼ tsp oregano
- ✓ ½ tsp ground cumin

Directions

Mix all ingredients together. Store in an air tight container.

Cooking Tips

To increase the heat substitute 1/2 tsp. crushed red pepper in place of the cayenne.

Chapter 13

Starches

Stage Number 1

Basic Polenta

Ingredients

- ✓ 3 cups water
- ✓ 1 tsp salt
- ✓ 1 cup yellow cornmeal
- ✓ 2 Tbs. ghee

Directions

Bring 3 cups of water to a boil in a heavy large saucepan. Add salt. Gradually whisk in the cornmeal. Reduce the heat to low and cook until the mixture thickens and the cornmeal is tender, stirring often, about 12 to 15 minutes. Turn off the heat. Add the ghee and stir until melted.

Lightly oil a half sheet pan. Transfer the hot polenta to the prepared baking dish, spreading evenly to 3/4-inch thick. Refrigerate until cold and firm, about 2 hours.

Stage Number 1

Bean Thread Noodles

Bean Thread Noodles are made from mung beans and can be found in the Oriental section of your supermarket.

Ingredients

- ✓ 1 package bean thread noodles
- ✓ boiling water

Directions

In a large pan, pour boiling water over the noodles. Let soak for 10-15 minutes. Drain.

Top noodles with any flavorful sauce, or toss the noodles with assorted raw veggies and mayo for a salad.

Stage Number 1

Brown & Wild Rice Pilaf

Ingredients

- ✓ 1/2 cup uncooked brown rice
- ✓ 1/2 cup uncooked wild rice
- ✓ 1/2 cup finely chopped onions
- ✓ 1/2 cup diced celery
- ✓ 1/4 cup ghee
- ✓ 1/4 tsp sage
- ✓ 1/4 tsp dried marjoram
- ✓ 1/4 tsp dried thyme
- ✓ 3 cups stock
- ✓ sea salt
- ✓ freshly ground black pepper

Directions

Cook and stir in brown rice, wild rice, onion and celery in ghee until onion is tender.

Stir in sage, marjoram, thyme and stock.

Heat to boiling, stirring occasionally.

Pour into ungreased 1 1/2-quart casserole.

Cover tightly.

Bake in 350-degree oven until all liquid is absorbed, about 1 hour.

Serves 6

Stage Number 1

Fried Rice

Ingredients

- ✓ 1 ghee
- ✓ 2 eggs - beaten
- ✓ 1 tsp ghee
- ✓ 2 tsp sesame oil
- ✓ 2 tbs. Bragg's Amino Acids
- ✓ 1/4 cup chopped onion or
- ✓ 1/2 -1 tsp onion powder
- ✓ 2 cups basmati rice, cooked and cooled
- ✓ 1/2 cup frozen green peas and carrots

Directions

Melt 1 Tbs. ghee in skillet or wok.

Scramble eggs, breaking up the cooked eggs into small pieces.

Set aside.

Melt remaining ghee in skillet or wok.

Sauté onions for 3 minutes. Skip this step if you are using onion powder.

Add rice to the hot pan and cook for several minutes, stirring constantly. If using onion powder, add now.

Stir in Bragg's until color of rice is uniform. Be careful and don't add too much. Bragg's is very salty.

Stir in peas. Cook until warm.

Add eggs. Heat only until warm. Serve.

Serves 4

Stage Number 1

Fried Sweet Potato Chips

Ingredients

- ✓ Vegetable oil, for frying
- ✓ 2 large sweet potatoes, washed
- ✓ Cinnamon or cinnamon mixed with organic
- ✓ sucanat (only for Stage 2)

Directions

In a large sauce pan, heat oil to 350 degrees F.

Thinly slice potatoes into round disks, about 1/4-inch thick. Fry for 1 1/2 to 3 minutes, stirring frequently. Remove from oil and drain on a paper towel. Sprinkle with sugar, to taste.

Serves 4

Stage Number 1

Garlic Rice

Ingredients

- ✓ 2 Tbs. ghee
- ✓ 2 Tbs. minced garlic
- ✓ 2 cups brown basmati rice
- ✓ 4 cups chicken broth
- ✓ Salt, (optional), to taste
- ✓ Freshly ground black pepper, (optional), to taste

Directions

Heat the ghee in a large skillet and sauté the garlic and rice, stirring constantly, until lightly brown.

Add the chicken broth, salt, and pepper and stir. Bring to a boil, then reduce heat to simmer, cover, and cook for 50 minutes.

Serves 8

Stage Number 1

Green Onion Hash Brown Potatoes

Ingredients

- ✓ 2 or 3 large leftover baked potatoes
- ✓ 1 Tbs extra virgin olive oil
- ✓ 2 Tbs ghee
- ✓ 5 scallions, finely chopped, whites and greens
- ✓ salt
- ✓ freshly ground black pepper

Directions

Scoop cooked potatoes from shells and coarsely chop.

Heat a medium nonstick skillet over moderate heat. Add oil and butter to the pan.

When butter melts into the oil, add green onions and cook 1 minute. Add potatoes and cook, turning occasionally, until potatoes are crusted and golden and onions begin to brown at edges.

Stage Number 1

Mashed Sweet Potatoes

Ingredients

- ✓ 2 lbs sweet potatoes
- ✓ 1/2 cup coconut milk
- ✓ ¼ teaspoon stevia (NuStevia Powder or SweetLeaf Liquid)
- ✓ 3 Tbs ghee
- ✓ 1 Tbs maple syrup or honey
- ✓ pinch salt and pepper
- ✓ 1 tsp fresh thyme leaves, optional

Directions

Preheat the oven to 350° F.

Place the potatoes on a foil lined baking sheet and bake until tender and begins to ooze sugary syrup, about 1 hour and 15 minutes. Remove from the oven and let sit until cool enough to handle.

Cut the potatoes in half lengthwise and scoop out the flesh with a spoon into a large bowl. Add the cream, sugar, butter, syrup, salt and pepper, and thyme, if using and mix, mashing until the potato mixture is smooth. Cover to keep warm until ready to serve.

Serves 4

Stage Number 1

Saffron Rice

Ingredients

- ✓ 2 cup brown basmati rice
- ✓ 1 tsp saffron threads
- ✓ 3 Tbs. boiling water
- ✓ 6 Tbs. ghee
- ✓ 1 2-inch piece stick cinnamon
- ✓ 4 whole cloves
- ✓ 1 cup finely chopped onion
- ✓ 2 tsp salt
- ✓ 1/4 tsp cardamom, ground
- ✓ 4 cups water or chicken broth

Directions

Place the saffron in a small bowl and cover with 3 tablespoons of boiling water. Soak for 10 minutes.

Meanwhile, heat the ghee over moderate heat in a large 3 or 4 qt. stockpot.

Add the cinnamon and cloves and stir well. Add the onions and sauté for about 5 minutes.

Add the rice and stir for about 5 minutes.

Pour in the 4 cups of liquid, salt, and the cardamom. Bring to a boil over high heat.

Add the saffron and its soaking water. Stir gently.

Cover, reduce heat, and cook for 50 minutes. Fluff and serve hot.

Serves 6

Chapter 14

Tips & Tricks

Stage Number 1

Alcohol & Liqueur Substitutions

When making substitutions for alcohols, it is important to keep the volume of liquid in the recipe the same as originally called for. Depending on the recipe, apple juice, chicken broth, or chicken broth with a bit of lemon juice often makes a good substitution for wine.

When using flavored liqueurs, extracts can be substituted if you make up the balance of the liquid with water. For example, if a recipe calls for 2 tablespoons Grand Marnier you could use 1/2 teaspoon orange extract. Just be sure to get the same level of orange flavor. This may take some experimentation.

Stage Number 1

Fruit & Vegetable Wash

Ingredients

- ✓ 1 large lemon
- ✓ 1/3 cup hydrogen peroxide
- ✓ pinch of sea salt

Directions

To make an excellent veggie wash, first juice a large lemon. Then boil the peel in purified water for approximately 10 minutes to extract the oil from the lemon peel.

Strain the liquid into a spray bottle a clean spray bottle. This should be abut 2 cups of lemon water.

To the strained liquid, add 1/3 cup hydrogen peroxide, and a pinch of sea salt.

Spray this solution on fruits or veggies, leave for 1 minutes, then rinse.

If you are traveling, take some paper towels, fold them in a baby wipes container that has been thoroughly cleaned. Pour some of the liquid over the top of the paper towels until they are damp. Now you have a convenient produce "wipe."

One thing to keep in mind, if the produce is not organic all the rinsing in the world doesn't matter-the pesticides get in the actual fruit, and cannot be washed off. Thoroughly wash even organic produce, to avoid small parasites or residues from whoever handled it along the way.

Stage Number 1

Lemon or Lime Juice Cubes

Ingredients

- ✓ Lemons
- ✓ Limes

Directions

A very quick way to have fresh lemon or lime juice anytime is to purchase a large amount of lemons and limes, bring them home and wash well.

Cut in half and juice the lemons into one bowl and limes into another. Make sure there are no seeds in the juice.

Mark 2 ice cube trays - one with lemon & one with lime. Using a tablespoon, measure the juices into the properly marked trays - one tablespoon per hole. Pop into your freezer until well frozen.

Turn the cubes out onto a clean surface and then store in marked bags in your freezer. When you need a tablespoon of lemon or lime juice for a recipe - it's already to use in your freezer. Just grab a cube and throw it into your ingredients.

Stage Number 1

Omelet Kits

Ingredients

- ✓ 2 red peppers
- ✓ 1 green pepper
- ✓ 1-2 large sweet onions

Directions

Dice all of the produce into small pieces. Combine. Put into quart size freezer bags and freeze.

When you are ready for an omelet. Heat your skillet with a little oil or ghee and pour in the desired amount of the frozen pepper/onion mix. Cook for several minutes until softened and fragrant.

Beat 3 eggs in a small bowl. Pour over the top of the sautéed peppers and onions and cook as you would an omelet.

Stage Number 1

Pumpkin Seeds

Ingredients

- ✓ pumpkin seeds
- ✓ oil
- ✓ salt

Directions

Drying seeds and roasting seeds are two different processes.

To dry, carefully wash pumpkin seeds to remove the clinging fibrous pumpkin tissue. Pumpkin seeds can be dried in the sun, in a dehydrator at 115-120 degrees for 1 to 2 hours, or in an oven on warm for 3 to 4 hours. Stir them frequently to avoid scorching.

To roast, take dried pumpkin seeds, toss with oil (1 teaspoon per cup of seeds) and/or salt and roast in a preheated oven at 250 degrees for 10 to 15 minutes.

Stage Number 1

Ready To Use Ground Beef

Ingredients

- ✓ Ground Beef
- ✓ Salt
- ✓ Pepper
- ✓ Onion Powder

Directions

When I find a great deal on ground beef, I buy about 10 pounds. I then put it in the crock pot and some salt, pepper and onion powder to and cook on high for about 2 hours, stirring every 30 minutes to break up the pieces.

Once the beef has cooled, I package it into 1 pound portions in freezer bags, label it and store in the freezer.

Then all I have to do is grab out a bag, do a quick thaw in the microwave of through it in the pan or crock pot frozen and have the beginnings of a quick dinner.

Stage Number 1

Yogurt Cheese

For those who can tolerate yogurt, here is a simple way to create a "cream cheese" like byproduct that is much healthier for you.

Ingredients

✓   2 quarts plain yogurt

Directions

Place 4 layers of cheesecloth in a colander set over a bowl. Add the yogurt and let drain overnight in the refrigerator. The desired consistency is that of soft cream cheese.

Use as you would cream cheese in a recipe or add herbs for a nice spread.

Cooking Tips

I have also tied the cheesecloth bundle to a cabinet handle and left it hanging over a bowl for a few hours in a cool kitchen. The weight helps it to drain faster.

Stage Number 1

Yummy Chicken Stock

Ingredients

- ✓ 6 - 8 chicken legs
- ✓ 16 cups of water
- ✓ onions
- ✓ carrots
- ✓ celery
- ✓ 2 bay leaves
- ✓ salt and pepper

Directions

Take about 6 to 8 chicken legs and put them in you slow cooker with 16 cups of water. Add in several onions, quartered, carrots, celery, 2 bay leaves, salt and pepper. Cook on low for about 6 hours.

Strain the broth, once cooled, into freezer bags in 1 cup increments. Pull the meat off the bones and save for a quick dish later in the week.

Chapter 15

Vegetables

Stage Number 1

Acorn Squash Gone Hawaiian

Ingredients

- ✓ 1 large acorn squash
- ✓ 2 tsp cinnamon
- ✓ 1 tsp nutmeg
- ✓ 1/2 tsp allspice
- ✓ 1/2 tsp ginger
- ✓ 1/2 cup crushed pineapple in own juice, drained, if allowed

Directions

Preheat the oven to 350° degrees.

To prepare the squash, cut it in half and remove the seeds. Place each half, cut-side down, on a baking sheet brushed lightly with oil. Bake the squash for 45 to 60 minutes until soft and tender.

Turn the acorn squash over and scoop out all the squash. In a bowl, mix the squash with all the remaining ingredients. Place in a casserole dish and bake for 5 more minutes, until pineapple bubbles.

Serves 4

Stage Number 1

Crunchy Snow Pea Sauté

Ingredients

- ✓ 1 pound snow peas, trimmed & strings removed
- ✓ 2 green onions, sliced
- ✓ 1 clove garlic, minced
- ✓ 1/8 tsp black pepper
- ✓ 2 tbs olive oil
- ✓ 2 tbs Bragg's Amino Acids

Directions

Add all ingredients to a sauté pan and heat until the snow peas have softened slightly.

Stage Number 1

Eggplant and the Sea

Ingredients

- ✓ 2 large eggplant
- ✓ 1 tsp salt
- ✓ 5 Tbs ghee
- ✓ 1 (10-ounce) can minced clams, drained, juice reserved
- ✓ 1 cup rice cracker crumbs with no yeast or white corn tortilla chip crumbs
- ✓ 1/2 cup coconut milk

Directions

Preheat oven to 350°F.

Peel the eggplant and cut it into thin rounds.

Bring a pot of water to a boil. Add the salt, then the eggplant, and cook for 10 to 15 minutes, or until tender.

Drain the eggplant well and mash it with 3 tablespoons of the ghee.

In a greased casserole, layer the mashed eggplant, the clams, and the crumbs. Dot with the remaining 2 tablespoons of ghee.

Blend the milk with the reserved clam juice. Taste and add salt, if needed.

Pour mixture over the casserole, but be sure to use only enough liquid to fully saturate the dish, otherwise, the dish will become too soupy. Bake for 30 minutes.

Serves 4

Stage Number 1

Glazed Carrots with Shallots & Thyme

Ingredients

- ✓ 1 1/2 pounds baby carrots, peeled and trimmed
- ✓ 5 shallots, ends trimmed, peeled and cut in half or quarters
- ✓ 1 cup chicken broth
- ✓ 2 tbs ghee
- ✓ 2 tsp salt
- ✓ 1 tsp honey
- ✓ 1 tsp fresh thyme, chopped

Directions

Cut each carrot in half lengthwise and then again to form wedges. Put the carrots and shallots in a sauté pan and add enough broth to come halfway up the sides of the vegetables.

Add the ghee, salt and honey and bring to a boil over high heat.

Cover the pan with the lid slightly askew, reduce the heat to medium-high and cook at a steady boil, shaking the pan occasionally, until the carrots are tender but not soft about 8 to 10 minutes.

Uncover, add the thyme, and continue to boil until the liquid evaporates. Continue to cook the carrots and shallots over medium-high heat, stirring occasionally, until they begin to caramelize and turn golden brown, about 3 minutes.

Taste and season to your liking.

Stage Number 1

Grilled Asparagus with Lemon & Garlic

Ingredients

- ✓ 1 lb asparagus
- ✓ 3 Tbs olive oil
- ✓ 2 cloves garlic, finely minced
- ✓ 1 tsp grated lemon zest
- ✓ 1/4 tsp paprika
- ✓ Salt and freshly ground black pepper

Directions

Trim asparagus. In a small bowl, combine oil, garlic, zest and paprika and stir with a fork. Lay asparagus side by side and pierce on 2 wooden skewers to form a raft. Place rafts on the grill and brush with oil mixture. Cook to desired tenderness and season with salt and pepper.

Serves 4

Stage Number 1

Hoppin' John - It's A Southern Thing!

This is a traditional southern recipe served on New Year's Day. And, everyone's grandmother had her own special version.

Ingredients

- ✓ Tbs ghee
- ✓ 1 small onion, chopped
- ✓ 1 small red bell pepper, chopped
- ✓ 1 clove garlic, minced
- ✓ 2 cups black-eye peas, cooked
- ✓ 2 cups cooked rice
- ✓ salt
- ✓ freshly ground black pepper
- ✓ 8 sprigs fresh parsley, for garnish

Directions

Melt the ghee in a large skillet over medium heat. Add onion, bell pepper, and garlic.

Cook for 5 minutes. Add peas and rice and cook an additional 10 to 15 minutes.

Be careful not to overcook; this dish is best if the bell pepper and onion still have a crunch to them.

Season to taste with salt and pepper. Garnish with fresh parsley.

Serves 6

Stage Number 1

Indian-Style Vegetable Stir Fry

Ingredients

- ✓ 1 tsp safflower oil
- ✓ 1 tsp curry powder
- ✓ 1 tsp ground cumin seed
- ✓ 1/8 tsp red pepper flakes
- ✓ 1 tsp minced seeded jalapeño
- ✓ 2 cloves garlic, minced
- ✓ 3/4 cup red bell peppers, chopped
- ✓ 3/4 cup carrots, thinly sliced
- ✓ 3 cups cauliflower florets
- ✓ 1/2 cup water
- ✓ 1/2 tsp salt
- ✓ 2 tsp cilantro, finely chopped

Directions

Heat oil in large skillet. Add curry powder, cumin, and red pepper flakes. Cook and stir about 30 seconds.

Stir in the jalapeño pepper and garlic. Add bell pepper and carrots. Mix well. Add cauliflower and reduce heat to medium.

Stir in 1/4 cup of water. Cook and stir until the water evaporates. Add remaining water. Cover and cook about 8 to 10 minutes or until vegetables are crisp-tender, stirring occasionally.

Add salt. Mix well. Sprinkle with cilantro and garnish with additional red bell pepper, if desired.

Serves 6

Stage Number 1

Oven Dried Tomatoes

Ingredients

- ✓ 6 large ripe tomatoes
- ✓ 1/4 cup olive oil
- ✓ salt
- ✓ thyme, optional

Directions

Preheat the oven to 325°F.

Slice the tomatoes in half crosswise. Place the tomatoes on a baking sheet, cut side up. Drizzle the oil over the tomatoes.

Sprinkle with salt and thyme, as desired.

Bake for about 2 hours, until tomatoes are wrinkled on the outside but still somewhat moist in the center. Serve warm or cool.

You can store these covered with olive oil in a jar in the refrigerator.

Serves 6

Stage Number 1

Quick & Easy Refried Beans

Ingredients

- ✓ One 15 ½ ounce can pinto beans, drained and rinsed
- ✓ 3 Tbs extra-virgin olive oil
- ✓ 1/2 medium onion, chopped
- ✓ 4 cloves garlic, minced
- ✓ 1 tsp ground coriander
- ✓ 1/2 tsp ground cumin
- ✓ 2/3 to 1 cup chicken broth
- ✓ salt
- ✓ freshly ground black pepper
- ✓ 1 Tbs chopped fresh cilantro, optional

Directions

Reserve about a third of the beans. Mash the rest of the beans in a medium bowl with a large fork. Set aside.

Heat the oil in a medium skillet over medium-high heat. Add the onion, and cook until lightly browned, about 4 minutes. Add the garlic and continue to cook, stirring, until lightly browned. Add the spices and cook until fragrant about 1 minute.

Add the mashed beans and half the broth; cook, stirring frequently, until slightly thickened, about 5 minutes. Add the reserved beans and the enough of the remaining broth to loosen up the beans. Simmer until the beans are thick but not pasty, about 2 minutes more.

Season with salt and pepper to taste. Stir in the fresh cilantro, if desired, and serve.

Stage Number 1

Ratatouille

This is one of my favorite dishes. I use it as a side dish with chicken or steak. I use it as a main dish over rice. And, it is even better the next day, if there are any leftovers.

Ingredients

- ✓ 1/2 cup olive oil
- ✓ 2 medium onions, thinly sliced
- ✓ 2 cloves garlic
- ✓ 28 oz diced tomatoes with juice
- ✓ 4 green peppers, julienned
- ✓ 1 large eggplant, peeled and diced
- ✓ 3 medium zucchinis, sliced into 1/2 inch disks
- ✓ salt
- ✓ freshly ground black pepper

Directions

Prepare all the vegetables for cooking by slicing or dicing.

Heat a large skillet over medium heat. Add a little over half of the oil and the onion. Sauté until the onion is tender. Add the garlic and cook for just 1 minute. Remove the onion and garlic from the pan and set aside.

Layer the bottom of the skillet with the green peppers, salt and pepper and 1/4 of the onion-garlic mixture.

Then layer the eggplant, more salt and pepper and another 1/4 of the onion-garlic mixture.

Repeat with the zucchini, more salt and pepper and 1/4 of the onion-garlic mixture.

Finally add the tomatoes, more salt and pepper and the last of the onion-garlic mixture. Pour the reserved tomato juice over the top, along with the remaining olive oil.

Cover and simmer over very low heat for 40 to 50 minutes.

Uncover and cook an additional 10 minutes to reduce the amount of liquid.

Stage Number 1

Roasted Cauliflower

Even if you think that you don't like cauliflower, you have to try this recipe. The cauliflower becomes so sweet and tasty. I can eat an entire head by myself.

Ingredients

- ✓   1 head cauliflower
- ✓   1/4 - 1/3 cup olive oil
- ✓   1 tsp onion powder
- ✓   1/2 -1 tsp salt
- ✓   1/4-1/2 tsp pepper

Directions

Break the cauliflower into smaller pieces. Cut it if you need to. Put into a zip lock baggie. Pour olive oil into the bag. Shake onion powder, salt & pepper in the bag. Close the bag and shake.

Pour onto a baking sheet. Put into a preheated oven at 500°F and cook for 10 minutes. Turn and cook for another 15 minutes. You want the cauliflower to begin to caramelize on the outside.

Serves 4

Stage Number 1

Spicy Broccoli

Ingredients

- ✓ 1/4 cup safflower oil
- ✓ 2 tsp toasted sesame oil
- ✓ 6 cloves garlic, minced
- ✓ 1 lb broccoli florets
- ✓ 2 tsp soy sauce or Bragg's Amino Acids
- ✓ 1 tsp dried red pepper flakes

Directions

Heat both oils in a large skillet.

Add the garlic and sauté for 1 minute or until golden brown.

Add the broccoli and cook for about 5 minutes, until it is tender, but still a little crunchy.

Add the Bragg's and continue to cook for 1 minute. Toss to coat broccoli. Stir in the red pepper flakes and serve.

Stage Number 1

Tangy Brussels Sprouts

Even if you think that you don't like Brussels sprouts, you will love this recipe. My mom always cooked the frozen kind that tasted nasty. But, when my food choices were limited, I began to experiment with different veggies and came up with this. Everyone who tastes it, loves it!

Ingredients

- ✓ 3 lbs Brussels sprouts, I prefer the smaller ones
- ✓ 1/2 cup ghee or olive oil
- ✓ 3 limes, juiced
- ✓ salt
- ✓ freshly ground black pepper

Directions

Pull of any wilted or loose outside leaves. You can either cut the sprouts into quarters, or you can cut the sprouts in half and then lay them flat on a chopping block and cut each half into julienne strips. Wash well and dry. I like to use a salad spinner for this job.

Heat a large skillet over medium-high heat. Melt the ghee, then add the sprouts and sauté until tender, about 6 - 10 minutes. Season with the lime juice, salt & pepper.

Serves 4

Stage Number 1

Vegetables Fried in Brown Rice Batter

Ingredients

- ✓ 1 large egg
- ✓ 1 tsp safflower oil
- ✓ 2/3 cup rice milk, plain
- ✓ 1 cup freshly milled brown rice flour
- ✓ 1/4 tsp baking powder
- ✓ 1/4 tsp onion powder
- ✓ 1/2 tsp salt
- ✓ 1/4 tsp pepper
- ✓ 3 cups washed and dried vegetable pieces such as zucchini summer squash, baby eggplant, onions, cauliflower, etc.

Directions

For batter, mix wet and dry ingredients separately. Then combine.

Dip veggies into batter, shaking off excess. Fry veggies in hot oil until golden brown.

Drain on paper towels.

Stage Number 1

Zucchini Noodles

This is a great low-carb substitute for pastas.

Ingredients

- ✓ 4 large zucchinis
- ✓ 1 tb olive oil
- ✓ salt
- ✓ freshly ground black pepper

Directions

Using a vegetable peeler or mandolin, make long, thin noodles by peeling the zucchini lengthwise. Turn the zucchini as you go so that you are left with the center seeded core. Discard the core.

Heat a large sauté pan on medium. Add the olive oil and zucchini. Season with the salt and pepper. Sauté just until warmed.

Use as a side dish with fresh herbs, or use in place of pasta.

Serves 4

Chapter 16

Resources

Converting To Metrics

Weight Conversions

Imperial (US)	Metric
1 oz	28.4 g
8 oz	227.5 g
16 oz or 1 lb	455 g
2.2 lb	1 kg

Volume Conversions

Imperial (US)	Metric
1/4 tsp	1.25 ml
1/2 tsp	2.5 ml
3/4 tsp	3.75 ml
1 tsp	5 ml
1 tb	15 ml
1/4 cup	62.5 ml
1/2 cup	125 ml
3/4 cup	187.5 ml
1 cup	250 ml

Temperature Conversions

Fahrenheit	Celsius
160°	71°
175°	80°
200°	93°
225°	107°
250°	121°
275°	135°
300°	149°
325°	163°
350°	177°
375°	190°
400°	205°
425°	218°
450°	232°
475°	246°

****To convert from Fahrenheit to Celsius, use this formula:
$C = (F-32) \times 0.5555$

When a recipe states to "broil," that means to cook in the oven with the upper heating elements on which is ofter termed "grill" in other countries outside North America.

About Glori

Glori Winders is a wife, mother, minister, author, entrepreneur and speaker. She and Tim have been married since 1988 and are the very proud parents of two incredible children, Dulce & Joshua.

Tim and Glori became empty-nesters in 2013 and since then have become full-time travelers. What an experience to see the world while continuing to write and create new businesses. They are truly blessed.

In 1998. due to an over-growth of Candida in her body Glori experienced serious health issues. Out of sheer desperation she became a master at reinventing recipes so that they were allergen free. With encouragement from her husband Glori wrote her first cookbook, The Yeast Free Cooking Manual, over eight years ago. It has now sold in over 25 countries around the world and helped countless people regain their health while still enjoying delicious food.

Glori loves working with dietary restrictions and creating menus that are quick and easy yet mouthwatering! In all of her research, she has embraced the general guidelines of the Paleo diet focusing on organic meats, poultry and seafood, lots of fresh vegetables and fruit along with healthy fats. This diet is beneficial for those who suffer from auto-immune issues, diabetes, inflammation, are over-weight or have gluten intolerance.

With the release of her third cookbook, The Top 21 Quick & Easy Paleo Recipes, Glori is quickly becoming recognized as an expert in the field of writing healthy, easy to follow recipes that taste great but satisfy your cravings for comfort foods. Her ingredients are simple and usually readily available making this a great cookbook for anyone any where.

She also co-authored, The Dorm Room Diner, with her daughter, Dulce which highlights recipes that can be prepared with little time, in a small space using few appliances.

A Note From Glori

Thank you for reading my book. I do appreciate your comments! I am also grateful for positive reviews. Please, take a moment to leave me a comment or review my book at your retailer. Also make sure that you visit my YouTube Channel for some great videos. In fact several of the recipes from this cookbook are featured there.

YOU HAVE BEEN **GLORI**-FIED

Glori

Glori Winders, The31Woman

GloriWinders.com

Discover Other Titles by Glori

Yeast Free Cooking, 7th Edition

The Dorm Room Diner, with Dulce Taylor

40 Days to Becoming A More Treasured Wife, with Tim Winders

40 Days to Becoming A Better Husband, with Tim Winders

Connect With Glori

Friend me on Facebook: Quick And Easy Paleo

Subscribe to my blog: GloriWinders.com

Follow me on Pinterest: The31Woman

Check out my Videos on Youtube: The31Woman

My Special Gift To You

Free Shopping Guide

Never leave the Market with toxic or unhealthy foods again because you will be armed with Glori's Shopping Guide!

This simple carry along tri-fold tool will equip you with a "cheat sheet" list for:

1. The 8 "BEST" Beverages that you and your family should be drinking instead of unhealthy, sugary sodas and juices.

2. 18 Foods that should be purchased as Organic Food. HINT: Not all food is worth the extra price for the Organic label. PLUS...the 11 foods that are less impacted by pesticides, therefore, it is OK to purchase these as conventional OR non-Organic. Great list for those on a budget.

3. 29 High Antioxidant foods as well as a long list of "safe" foods that should be included in almost any diet or food plan.

4. 25 foods that you should NEVER NEVER under any circumstances purchase and bring in to your home.

Download Your Free Shopping Guide at

http://gloriwinders.com/shopping-guide.html

Made in the USA
Middletown, DE
04 January 2016